SOCIETATI·REGIAE·LONDINI
GULIELMUS·HAMILTON
BALN·ORD·EQUES·
D·D·D·
CIƆIƆCCLXXIX·

CONTENTS

VOLCANOES
FIRE FROM THE EARTH

Maurice Krafft

DISCOVERIES

HARRY N. ABRAMS, INC., PUBLISHERS

Volcanoes tremble, rumble, explode, and rip themselves apart. For centuries people around the world were powerless to understand the earth's convulsions. Looking for explanations, they conjured up stories of superhuman forces. Surprisingly, groups of people who knew nothing of each other developed similar legends.

CHAPTER I
MYTHS AND LEGENDS

The earliest evidence of human interest in volcanic phenomena is this c. 6000 BC wall painting (right) of an erupting volcano, probably Hasan Dag (in central Turkey). Opposite: Eight thousand years later, in 1789, French revolutionaries used the liberating force of an erupting volcano as a symbol in their call for the destruction of monarchies.

"In a Single Dreadful Day and Night...the Island of Atlantis Was...Swallowed Up by the Sea"

Volcanic activity has given rise to one of the most enduring of all legends, that of Atlantis. In two of his dialogues, the *Critias* and the *Timaeus*, Greek philosopher Plato (c. 428–348 BC) told of the sudden disappearance of a vast island and its inhabitants, the Atlanteans. According to Plato the Atlanteans were refined people who admired works of art, venerated bulls, built sumptuous palaces, and extolled social justice. Their civilization was said to be as powerful and prosperous as that of pharaonic Egypt. But, suddenly, everything collapsed.

In May 1967 Greek archaeologist Spyridon Marinatos discovered on Thera, the main island of the Santorin island group, a Minoan town, Akrotiri, buried under several feet of pumice ejected during the eruption of 1620 BC. He uncovered streets, houses decorated with frescoes (opposite below: *The Crocus Picker*), and hundreds of pottery vessels and utensils.

Work by archaeologists and geologists has produced the hypothesis that Atlantis, if it ever existed, was located on the volcanic island of Santorin (Thera) in the Aegean Sea. Here, around 1620 BC, a tremendous succession of volcanic explosions, some of them rising almost 30 miles into the air, opened an enormous crater in the middle of the island. It was the greatest volcanic cataclysm of the last three millennia. A colossal tidal wave, about 100 feet high, swept southward along the coasts of Crete and the whole

Above left: A fresco of boats from Akrotiri.

In 197 BC a small volcano was born in Santorin: Kameni, the "burned land." Above: An aerial view showing Kameni active in 1866.

eastern Mediterranean. Santorin itself was covered by a layer of pumice fragments up to 100 feet deep. Over a foot of ash fell in Turkey, several hundred miles away!

Given the many similarities between the Santorin eruption and the story of the disappearance of Atlantis, it is likely that the legend was based on an actual event.

Other Legends Also Had Their Historical Origins in the Santorin Eruption

The story of the flood of Deucalion in Greek mythology—in which Poseidon, god of the sea, took his revenge on Zeus by inundating Attica, Argolis, the Gulf of Salonika, Rhodes, and the whole Mediterranean coast from Lycia (now Turkey) to

Above: Ruins in Akrotiri, Santorin. Only a small part of the town has been excavated.

Sicily—was also probably inspired by the tidal wave caused by the eruption on Santorin. In another tale, when the Argonauts (Jason's companions in the quest for the Golden Fleece) were preparing to cast anchor at Dicte, Thalos, a bronze giant, "threw blocks of stone at them," but Medea overcame the monster, "whose blood began to flow like molten lead and who fell with a great cracking." Then, "a terrible veil shrouded the sea." Might not the blocks of stone, the molten lead, the terrible cracking, and the veil shrouding the sea be the lava flows, earthquakes, and ash falls of the Santorin eruption?

Vulcan—Vulcano—Volcanoes

For the ancient Greeks, Sicilian volcano Etna's activities were the work of Hephaestus, the god of fire who, hammering on his anvil amid smoke and sparks, forges beneath the earth the weapons of the gods. The Romans called him Vulcan, preferring to see his abode in the bowels of Hiera (present-day Vulcano) in the Aeolian (now Lipari) Islands. Vulcano gave its name to volcanoes—in the ancient world, they were called either *etna* or *hiera*.

Hephaestus was not alone in his underground forge; his companions in labor were the Cyclops, giants whose single eyes recall the circular shape of Etna's glowing crater. As they beat iron to shape Zeus'

This aerial view of the island of Vulcano (1782, left) by Jean Houel unintentionally evokes the eye of a Cyclops, one of the giants who helped Hephaestus-Vulcan (below) to fashion Apollo's bronze arrows, Hercules' invisible armor, and Achilles' shield.

According to the account of ancient Roman poet Virgil, the giant Enceladus was buried beneath Etna by the goddess Athena in punishment for rebelling against the gods. Opposite: A 17th-century depiction. Earthquakes are his tossing, rumblings are his plaintive and imploring voice, and eruptions are his burning, flaming breath. Mimas, his brother, was said to be buried under Vesuvius by Hephaestus. The blood of other defeated giants wells up beneath the Phlegraean (Blazing) Fields (a volcanic region near Naples, Italy).

scepter in their furnaces beneath Etna, fire leapt out of the volcano, sometimes with such force that it annihilated nearby villages.

Volcanoes: Homes to Gods and Demons

Easily offended, these immortal beings torment the living, taking vengeance for imagined insults, unleashing their lightning on unfortunate mortals, and only rarely coming to their aid.

In the Pacific's "ring of fire"—a great circle of volcanoes extending from the west coasts of North, Central, and South America to Japan, Malaya, the South Seas islands, and New Zealand—such beliefs abound. All of Japan's great volcanoes are sacred and surrounded by temples. The most famous of the volcanoes, Fujiyama, a symbol of purity and eternity, is the kingdom of a sun god.

In southern Peru the evil spirit of the volcano called El Misti, whose tantrums ravaged the city of Arequipa several times, was punished by a sun god who plugged his crater with ice.

Elsewhere it was the god of fire who was said to reign in volcanoes. Northwest Coast Indians say that the

Ngauruhoe (above left), a crater in New Zealand, is named for Ngatoro, a sorcerer, and Auruhoe, his favorite female slave, who died of cold on its summit.

According to Wyoming legend, 865-foot-high Devil's Tower (left), a lava formation, sprang up to save seven little girls being chased by a giant bear. The vertical striations are the bear's claw marks.

evil fire god lives in Mount Mazama and the good snow god in Mount Shasta (both mountains are in the Cascades). One day the rival gods began to fight. At the end of a long, hard struggle the fire god was defeated and decapitated. As a sign of his defeat, a great expanse of water, Crater Lake, filled the cavity of Mount Mazama. (The crater was actually formed 6000 years ago, during an eruption.)

Volcanic Love Stories

According to legend, volcanoes love and suffer like humans. In New Zealand, Taranaki (present-day Mount Egmont) and Ruapehu both fell in love with the fair Tongariro (Ngauruhoe) in a classic example of the love triangle. Taranaki threw himself upon his rival who, to defend himself, poured down showers of boiling water taken from his crater-lake. The attacker replied with showers of stones that destroyed the

Above: The perfect cone of Fujiyama, glorified in this print by Katsushika Hokusai, was reputedly the work of a giant. Wanting to fill in the Pacific Ocean, he worked for a whole night loading sacks with earth in Asia to empty them into the ocean. At dawn, seeing that he had made little progress in his ambitious project, he decided to abandon it and threw down his last load on Japan, where it became sacred Fujiyama.

summit of Ruapehu's cone. Ruapehu swallowed, melted, and then spat the stones out over Taranaki, who was burned and fled to the sea to nurse his wounds. The valley of the Wanganui River marks his course. Defeated, he withdrew far from his enemy. But the native Maori still refuse to live on the Egmont-Ruapehu axis, sure that one day the fight will begin again.

Punishing the Negligent

Once every hundred years a great ceremony takes place in the Hindu temple of Besakih, at the foot of the volcano Agung, in Bali. But in 1963 the rites that opened the festival had, it seems, been botched by the priests. The vengeance of the gods was terrible, and the volcano—which had been dormant for six centuries—awoke: 1184 people died in the ash and mud. Today, some believers are sure that another cataclysm will occur during the next centenary ceremony of Besakih.

Human Sacrifice to Appease Volcanoes

In Nicaragua some peoples sacrificed their loveliest young virgins by casting them into the lava lake of Masaya. In nearby El Salvador the people who live near Lake Ilopango attributed the 1879–80 eruption beneath the lake to the fury of the goddess who lived there. She was said to be angry because the government had put a boat into service on the lake. The sacrifice of a young child, bound hand and foot and thrown into the lake, appeased the goddess.

According to the Aztecs, eruptions in Mexico (above, Popocatépetl) were caused by European conquistadors profaning their temples. In Nicaragua beautiful girls were thrown into the lava lake of Masaya as a sacrifice to the gods (left).

The 1886 cataclysm of Tarawera in New Zealand (opposite) buried three villages and killed over a hundred people. The Maori had two explanations for this punishment by the gods: Either the villagers had eaten wild honey (which was taboo), or they had become degenerate through contact with Europeans.

The Conversion of Volcanoes to Christianity

"Smoke rose from his nostrils, and a devouring fire came out of his mouth; blazing coals sprang out of it...." Yahweh, god of the Hebrews, bears a strange resemblance to a volcano. According to the Bible, he "rained upon Sodom and upon Gomorrah brimstone and fire." All these volcanic manifestations are associated with the notion of eternal fire, or Gehenna, the hell of biblical texts.

In 1104 a violent eruption shook Hekla in southwest Iceland. The most horrible stories circulated in the Christian world: Might this be the mouth of hell? Over a hundred years earlier in Iceland, the Vikings' parliament, the Althing, gathered at Thingvellir, a vast expanse of lava ruptured by fissures, where tall basalt cliffs provided exceptional acoustics. One important question was on the agenda: Should the Vikings adopt Christianity or continue to venerate the Nordic gods? The debate was lively, with each clan trying to invalidate the other's arguments. Suddenly, a messenger arrived, announcing that lava was pouring from a fissure and threatening the village of Chief Thórodd. The pagans were jubilant: "This is not surprising. Our gods are angered by your proposals, Christians...." But Chief Snorri, a supporter of Christianity, turned the news to his advantage. Indicating the vast expanse of congealed lava that covers the valley of Thingvellir, he asked: "And who were they angry at when this lava poured out?" (At that time, there had been no Christianity on the island.) Snorri won the debate. And that is how, because of a lava flow, the Vikings of Iceland were converted.

In 1600, in Peru, the awakening of Omate plunged the town of Arequipa, over 40 miles away, into a terrifying darkness caused by the

fall of ash. Christians believed the end of the world had arrived and the eruption was the expression of divine anger against the sins of humanity. Illegitimate couples got married, and debtors settled their accounts. The non-Christian Indians saw in it the revolt of their volcano against the Spaniards. They, too, believed it was the end of the world and killed sheep, chickens, and pigs and held great orgies while awaiting death. The Indians were astonished that the other nearby volcano, El Misti, did not awake to help Omate chase the colonists away. But they quickly found an explanation: El Misti had become Christian, and the Spanish had baptized it San Francisco.

If such stories seem old and quaint, it is worth remembering that the enormous explosion of Mount Saint Helens, in the state of Washington on 18 May 1980, was interpreted by some Adventist preachers as a punishment from God and a warning to those who swear and drink alcohol.

Above: Thingvellir, the Vikings' meeting place. Opposite: Detail of a 1585 map of Iceland.

"From the bottomless abyss of Hekla, or rather from Hell itself, rise melancholy sobs and hoarse groans; these lamentations can be heard for miles around…. If people are waging war somewhere in the world, then terrible howls, weeping, and gnashing of teeth can be heard in the mountain."
Caspar Peucer

S Maria ob Aretia

Nowws<us

Christianity and Volcanoes Were Most Closely Connected at Etna and Vesuvius

Miracles wrought by the patron saints of the cities at the feet of these two volcanoes in Italy were the only hope of stopping the threat of eruptions. St. Agatha protects the city of Catania, at the foot of Mount Etna, and St. Januarius looks after Naples, which lies below Vesuvius.

At Etna, the first miracle took place on 5 February 253, a year after the martyrdom of Agatha at Catania. Seeing that the lava was advancing toward their city, the inhabitants presented to the approaching flow the

Every time Vesuvius erupts, St. Januarius (above, in a 1633 engraving) is recalled. In 1660 he rained down little black crosses on the villages around the volcano. A miracle! In fact, these were twin pyroxene crystals shaped like a cross (left), torn from the molten rock and hurled out of the crater. The next year, another miracle: A comet, represented by an eagle (opposite), passed through the sky.

Vorago

Sarnum fl.

Boscus

Scafatum fl.

Pompeji

Torre...

Canon...

veil that covered the
saint's sepulcher. The lava
separated and stopped. During
the volcano's activity in 1669, they again called on the
help of St. Agatha's relics, but with less success—a
third of Catania was engulfed. In 1971 the villagers of
San Alfio, carrying the relics of their own patron saint,
knelt before the blocks of lava to beg to be spared.
Their wish was granted.

In Naples every great eruption of Vesuvius calls for
a procession of the relics of St. Januarius. The register
that records these ceremonies enabled British diplomat
and archaeologist Sir William Hamilton
(1730–1803) to draw up a chronology
of the volcano's activities.

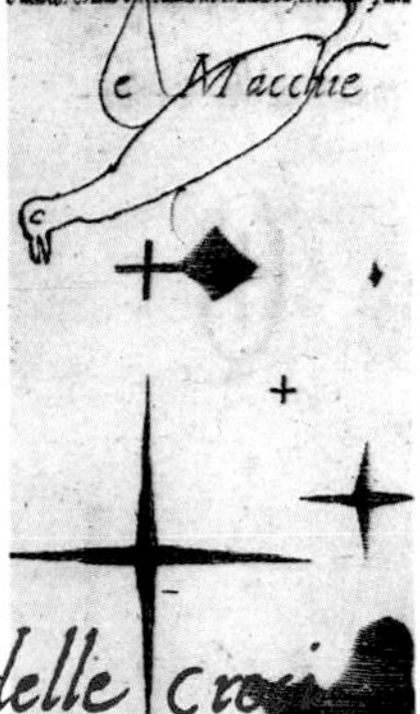

...ura Cometa nel regno di Capricorno con la c...
...tto piedi: endo poi sempre scemando talmente, che...
...sempre fu pallida e saturnino, et il lume smorto. il...
...colore. Cristo offeruola in Bauiera, Boemia Fan...

e Macchie

Forme delle croci

N aples, late 19th century (left): Peasants invoke St. Januarius as their protector. Armed with studded whips, some penitents flagellated themselves until they bled; others wept and tore their hair; women carried crosses; the monks covered their heads with ashes and recited psalms. All of this human river converged on the cathedral. There, from his balcony, the archbishop showered down blessings and absolutions and exposed the relics of the saint to make Vesuvius stop. A similar scene from 1906 is depicted above. The Catholic clergy no longer associates volcanoes with Hell, but when Vesuvius next awakes, the statue of St. Januarius will undoubtedly put in another appearance.

Astonishingly Potent Beliefs

The memory of the birth of the volcano Parícutin in a Mexican cornfield on 20 February 1943 is still the pretext for an annual pre-Easter pilgrimage to the site of the village that was destroyed by the volcano.

Human sacrifices have ceased, but only a few years ago in Japan lonely old people, jilted lovers, and ruined businessmen were still killing themselves by jumping into the active crater on the island of O-shima, south of Tokyo. Every year crowds of pilgrims seeking purity climb Aso, Ontake, and especially Fujiyama, leaving offerings in the temples that line the way up. Great

Only the facade and choir of the basilica of San Juan Parangaricutiro (above) in Mexico withstood Parícutin's lava flows.

Shinto ceremonies open and close the seasons when the sacred volcanoes may be climbed.

During the annual festival of Kesodo, thousands of Indonesians come to the edge of the crater of the Bromo volcano, in eastern Java, to pray and throw in offerings of coins, fruit, flowers, rice, and chickens.

The Pacific's Most Famous Volcanic Divinity

The goddess Pelé was born in Tahiti, but was chased away by her sister Namakaokahai after a quarrel. Her long flight ended at Hawaii, in Halemaumau, the crater of Kilauea, which is where she now lives. Pelé unleashes all the island's eruptions. Very quick-tempered, she opens up craters with a simple kick of her heel and hurls lava on her detractors. Before each

Most Indonesian volcanoes are sacred. Merapi, on Java, belongs to the sultan; a guardian even possesses a symbolic key to it. Once a year, a priest climbs to the volcano's summit, where he places objects and clothes belonging to the sultan. Even today, at Semeru and Guntur, other volcanoes in Java, wise men dressed all in white, carrying no metallic objects, indicating nonaggression, come to meditate at the edge of the craters in the cold and the clouds. A 19th-century lithograph of Guntur is below.

eruption she appears in the guise of a wrinkled old woman or, more rarely, a very beautiful girl.

Legends about Pelé abound, often linked to real eruptions. For example, it is said that one day she fell in love with two young chiefs from eastern Hawaii who were champions of *holua*, a sled used on grassy slopes. She appeared in the form of a magnificent princess and joined them in sledding, at which she excelled. But the two men recognized her and fled. Furious, she stamped her foot on the ground, which trembled, heated up, and vomited rivers of lava over the whole region. The chiefs ran to the sea, but the flow engulfed them, and they perished. Along the coast, two flattened cones, Na Puu a Pelé (the Hills of Pelé), are said to represent the petrified corpses of the unlucky heroes.

Legend and Geological Observation

The story of the two *holua* champions recalls a very real event, an eruption in which lava flows entered the sea. The contact between water and molten rock was explosive and produced the two cones. Similarly, the underground route that Pelé is

Hawaiians in ceremonial costumes gather at the edge of Kilauea to honor Pelé (above left). Belief in her supernatural powers was shaken in the 19th century when Kapiolani, the Christian wife of an island chief, deliberately provoked the goddess by throwing stones into the lava lake (above right). Pelé did not respond, so many Hawaiians concluded that she was only a myth and became converts to Christianity.

supposed to use to reach her abode in the crater of Kilauea on the coast corresponds to the route of molten rock (magma) inside the volcano.

One last legend summarizes the geological history of the Hawaiian archipelago: Trying to escape her sister, Pelé swam from island to island, punctuating her flight with craters— Diamond Head on Oahu, Haleakala on Maui, and Kilauea on Hawaii. This progression matches the age of the volcanoes, which are younger and younger as one travels southeast.

In Hawaii, as elsewhere, volcanic divinities are formidable rivals to volcanologists. It is now up to the latter to give their version of volcanism and its origins.

Pelé's presence is felt so strongly that some Hawaiians still see her face in the lava fountains and her body in the flows (above and opposite).

Scholars in ancient times thought that volcanoes and earthquakes were due to hurricanes blowing in underground cavities —causing the cavities' walls to vibrate (earthquakes) and igniting fires that pour out over the surface of the earth (volcanoes). Ever since, volcanology has struggled to free itself from such ideas.

CHAPTER II
EARLY THEORIES

Pompeii and Herculaneum were buried, along with at least 2000 victims, in AD 79. Left: A 19th-century Russian painting of the Pompeii disaster. Eighteen centuries later, the archaeologist Giuseppe Fiorelli (1823–96) poured plaster into the hollows left by the bodies buried in the ash to create casts such as the one at right.

Over the centuries countless theories about volcanic activity have been advanced—some based on direct observation, and others purely speculative. The first interpretation of the theory of volcanic action (volcanism) comes to us from Thales, a Greek mathematician of the 6th century BC. The Babylonians, Phoenicians, and Hebrews may have tried to advance explanations before him, but their theories have not survived. Thales imagined that all terrestrial convulsions are caused by water—the earth was a disk floating on an ocean that unleashes earthquakes with every storm. His pupil Anaximander (610–c. 547 BC) believed that a superior natural force produced both heat and cold, and that mixing them produced fire.

In the 5th Century BC the Ancient World's Two Key Words for Explaining Volcanic Action Were Established: Wind and Fire

Greek tragedian Aeschylus (525–456 BC) alluded to an eruption of Etna, that of 479 BC. The poet Pindar (518–438 BC) also described an activity of the volcanic giant. "From the mountain pure springs of unapproachable fire are vomited from the inmost depths...." In ancient lore Etna is the pillar of the sky spewing out the waters that the sea pours into the whirlpool of the monster Charybdis.

Empedocles (c. 490–30 BC), another Greek philosopher, declared that the world is ruled by four elements, which he called the "roots of all things": underground fire,

Wind plays an essential role in early interpretations. Two 19th-century depictions of Etna (opposite) suggest the intensity of the wind gusts.

Empedocles (below, in a fresco by Luca Signorelli) was more pragmatic in his description of Etna's flows: "Masses of fire advance; before them they roll pell-mell shapeless pieces of rock, clouds of black sand fly up with a crash.... A tranquil river lets its waves flow out.... Nothing can stop the fiery surge, no dam could contain it."

water, air, and earth. He sat down on the slopes of Etna to absorb the volcano's mysteries by meditation. In despair at finding no answers to his questions, he is said to have thrown himself into the crater.

Plato Traveled to Sicily to See Etna

According to Plato, the "underground regions communicate through numerous channels" where "there flow inexhaustible rivers of hot and cold waters." In the depths of the earth, an enormous winding river of fire, the Pyriphlegethon, feeds the volcanic craters. He was the first to describe the genesis of lava: "Sometimes, when the earth has melted because of fire, and then cooled again, a black-colored stone is formed."

As for Aristotle (384–322 BC), he compared the earth to an organism that is born, lives, and dies. Its convulsions—earthquakes and volcanoes—are bouts of fever accompanied by gasping and spasms. Underground fire is caused by "the air being broken into particles which burst into flames from the effects of the shocks and friction of the wind when it plunges into narrow passages." He gave the name *crater* (Greek for *cup*) to the depression at the top of a volcanic cone.

The Greek geographer Strabo (58 BC–AD 21) knew that Vesuvius was of volcanic origin. Yet, at the time, the volcano was in a profound sleep, and covered in vegetation up to its summit. "[Vesuvius] possesses craters of fire which go out only when they lack fuel."

The explanations of volcanism put forward by most Greek philosophers were based on speculation rather than observation. An exception was the historian Poseidonius (c. 135–c. 51 BC); he described eruptions, hot springs, and volcanic landscapes with the eye of a trained scientist. His writings have not come down to us, but Strabo knew them and transcribed his observations; they are precious documents for volcanology. Strabo describes several eruptions at sea, especially that of 126 BC, off Panarea in the Lipari Islands, and the birth of the island of Hiera in 197 BC,

ORIENS.

A
Ex hortum montium Terra ac lapidibus Sulphur conficitur.
B
Ex hisce albicantibus magna fit copia aluminis.
C
Aqua hic est perennis nigra æ- pecta et crassa ita feruida vt ouum cruduin intinctum coctū etrudatur; si mare coestuat vsq. ad 24. palmas chulio sese attollitur.

DVM EXPENDAR.

in the middle of the Santorin caldera (a huge crater). As he put it, it "rose up as if on springs."

Transcribing an incident referred to in Plato's dialogue the *Timaeus*, Strabo also relates an eruption at Ischia, in the Bay of Naples, which was accompanied by a tidal wave: "The sea retired from it to a distance of three stadia, but after remaining so for a short time it returned and inundated the island, thus extinguishing the fire [of the volcano]."

Strabo named the Solfatara (a volcanic vent in the Phlegraean Fields, above) Forum Vulcani—aptly expressing its origin.

A 17th-century depiction of Plato's Pyriphlegethon (opposite).

The earthquake of AD 62, perhaps signaling the eruption of 79, destroyed numerous monuments in Pompeii, including the Temple of Jupiter, shown in a bas-relief at left.

But Strabo was also a great observer himself and a tireless traveler. He described the volcanic Lipari Islands—Lipari, with its "hot springs" and its "smoky blazes"; Vulcano, "the blazing," with its "three breaths, coming as if from three craters"; Strongyla, "the round"; Stromboli, "deficient in the force of the flames which are emitted, but their brightness is greater"— and also Vesuvius.

A Long Poem, *Aetna,* Summarizes Roman Concepts of Volcanism in a Very Picturesque Way

In the course of the 643 lines devoted to Etna, the poet—probably Virgil (70–19 BC)—described the volcano and depicted the different phases of an eruption. Roman scholars were less fond of pure speculation than the Greeks and sought rational explanations for nature's phenomena. Lucretius (98–55 BC), also a poet, claimed that Etna was a completely hollow mountain in which a violent underground wind circulated near sea level. The flames produced by the wind came to the surface through "rectilinear fissures." This was the first allusion to tectonics, the study of the earth's crust.

Shortly afterward, Ovid (43 BC–AD 17) stated that Etna evolves by "modifying its respiratory tracts," closing one cavity and opening another. He specified that volcanic activities stop when "the earth gives the flame no more nourishment or fatty foods; then, since voracious nature does not tolerate hunger, the fire abandons the place."

In the same century, Vitruvius explained that

it was "sulfur, alum, and bitumen" that fed "the deep heat of the fires." An architect, he was interested in the pumice and pozzolanas (porous volcanic ash) of the area near Vesuvius, showing how useful they were for making fast-setting cements.

On 5 February AD 62 a Violent Earthquake Shook Campania

Seneca (4 BC–AD 65), tutor of the Roman emperor Nero, was very observant and made many references to earthquakes. He expressed

This Pompeian fresco, the oldest known depiction of Vesuvius, shows the volcano Monte Somma, with Bacchus, god of wine, at its foot. Strabo was the first to recognize the mountain's volcanic nature. He was an innovator in several ways, especially in claiming that volcanoes that are frequently active—and whose underground force is thus released little by little—do not undergo major eruptions: This idea is still current today. According to Strabo, volcanoes are the planet's safety valves. He noticed that the "black

mud," the term he used for the lava flowing on Etna, congealed and became "mill-stone." He also discovered that volcanic ash rapidly becomes very fertile: "The roots produced by the districts covered with these ashes are so good for fattening sheep that they sometimes choke on them."

two new concepts of volcanism that are still true today. First, he stressed the importance of the gases and vapors that the "underground fires excite, tightening the springs of the blast" until "the explosion"—he had discovered the principle of gas pressure as the motive force of eruptions. Second, he explained that the fire in every case was fed by an individual local source, a kind of reservoir located under each volcano.

In specifying that it was magma, rather than fire, that came out of volcanoes, the philosopher Philo of Alexandria (13 BC–AD 54) became a distant precursor of Plutonism, a theory that would not be put forward seriously until the 18th century!

The letters of Pliny the Younger contain meticulous descriptions of many phenomena associated with Vesuvius' eruptions: The earth tremors before the awakening; the enormous vertical column of ash and gas in the shape of an Italian parasol pine and crossed by lightning (a "Plinian plume"); the falls of volcanic dust and pumice that bury buildings and fill people's lungs; the total darkness; the toxic sulfurous gases; the ceaseless earthquakes that rend houses apart; the hot ash-flows and horizontal blasts; and the tidal waves that follow abrupt upheavals of the ground.

Seventeen Years Later, Vesuvius Annihilated Pompeii

In his enormous encyclopedia of thirty-seven volumes, *Natural History*, Pliny the Elder (AD 23–79) drew up a list of all the active volcanoes then known to exist—they barely amounted to ten. According to him, just before the eruptions are unleashed there are earthquakes, but the air is extremely calm and the sea quiet, because the winds have already plunged into the earth and are preparing to reemerge: the calm before the storm.

Vesuvius' 1822 eruption, from an 1862 lithograph.

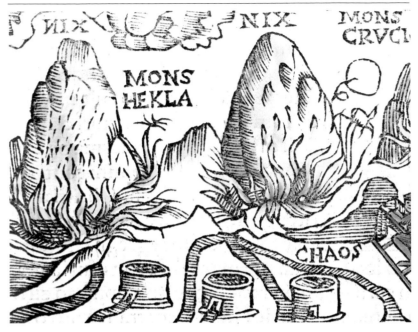

Such a storm was to kill him on 24 August AD 79, when Vesuvius awoke after a very long sleep. His nephew, Pliny the Younger (AD 62–114), who became history's first volcanologist, relates the event in two letters. They represent crucial documents in volcanology, the first detailed eyewitness descriptions of a cataclysmic eruption.

The Middle Ages Neglected Volcanoes

In Europe knowledge of volcanoes was confined to the monasteries and a few scholars, such as the Byzantine historian Procopius who wrote, around 580, that "after Vesuvius had spat out its ashes, the harvests of the neighboring countryside were abundant." An anonymous Benedictine monk, relating the voyage of St. Brendan in the same century, described an eruption, probably of Hekla in Iceland: "A smoky and foggy land, stinking worse than carrion...throws fire and

Hekla (above, in a 16th-century print) is one of Iceland's most active volcanoes. Since its eruption in 1104 it has awakened 167 times, most recently in January 1991. The hydrofluoric acid contained in its gases and ashes contaminates pastures and poisons livestock. Its activities often begin with an explosive phase of a few hours, followed by impressive lava flows which generally last several weeks.

flames, blazing beams and scrap iron, pitch and sulfur up to the clouds, then everything falls back into the abyss." Judas, he said, was imprisoned there.

It appears that it was in the 12th century that the word *volcano* acquired the meaning it has today. The English naturalist Alexander Neckam (1157–1217) used it to describe places where the earth's fire burns. A century later Albertus Magnus (c. 1207–80) invented the first experimental model of a volcano: a bronze vase with two plugged orifices, filled with water brought to the boiling point over a fire. The pressure of the water vapor would explode either the upper cork, releasing a gassy plume, or the lower one, projecting boiling water onto the fire, which would suddenly eject embers and hot ash around the hearth.

The Theories of the Ancients Were Rediscovered

The creation of many universities and the invention of the printing press in the 15th century led to a tremendous diffusion of knowledge throughout Europe. The Church, sensing a threat to its power, imposed its censorship on every published work. Writings had to conform to Holy Scripture and respect the notions of Hell and of the Flood. This prohibition had to be obeyed—or evaded.

On 28 September 1538 a volcano rose

"On the 27th and 28th of last September, earth tremors were felt continually, night and day, in the town of Pozzuoli…. On the 29th, the earth opened near the lake and presented an awful mouth which furiously vomited smoke, fire, stones…. The stones were turned to pumice by the devouring flames, and the size of some of them exceeded that of an ox."

Pietro Giacomo de Toledo, 1539

Pietro Giacomo de Toledo was present in 1538 at the birth of Monte Nuovo in the Phlegraean Fields. Below: A contemporary depiction of the event.

De conflagratione

During the eruption of Monte Nuovo, the Solfatara (which owes its name to the sulfur crystals that were deposited as fumes and gas were emitted), less than 3 miles away, apparently showed no signs of being reactivated. Volcanic sulfur used to be collected for making gunpowder, illustrated here (left) in a 15th-century manuscript.

Volcanoes are born in the ocean's depths far more often than on land. Iceland, Italy, Greece, the Canary Islands, and the Azores have all witnessed several marine eruptions that created short-lived islands. One of these (below) emerged in 1638 off San Miguel, in the Azores.

out of the ground in Italy's Phlegraean Fields, near Naples. It was christened the Monte Nuovo. When the eruption declined a week later, the "new mountain" was over 450 feet high. Scholars all over Europe realized the significance of this event and would cite it as proof of the rapid formation of the earth's mountains and geological layers.

The 16th Century Witnessed Great Discoveries Overseas

For a decade Masaya, in present-day Nicaragua, offered the spectacle of a lake of lava boiling at the bottom of a crater. Several Spanish historians described the phenomenon in great detail, but their writings passed unnoticed by the scientific world. The activity of São Jorge, in the Azores in 1580, was also little heard

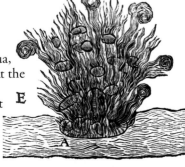

of. But for the first time, witnesses there had described
ardente nuvem, or *nuées ardentes,* clouds of hot ash and
rock, now often known as ash flows.

There were still very few scientists who buckled down
to research in the field or to experimentation. Petrus
Severinus, a professor of literature, meteorology, and
medicine, rebelled against this attitude in 1571: "Burn
your books, put on your shoes, climb mountains,
explore deserts to gain for yourselves some idea of the
things of nature. Buy coal, make furnaces, observe and
try out experiments, and never give up."

German, Swiss, and Italian Scholars Gave Their Interpretations

German Georg Bauer (1494–1555), better known as
Georgius Agricola, the father of mineralogy, attacked
the theory of the astronomers of the period who
attributed the earth's underground fire—and hence
earthquakes and volcanoes—to the rays of the sun
penetrating to the depths of our planet. He believed it
was vapor under pressure that caused the inflammation
of sulfur and "mountain oil," just as clouds caused
lightning. He brought back into usage the term *basalt,*
which had been coined by Pliny the Elder for a type of
rock in Ethiopia. Basalt, wrote the Swiss Konrad von
Gesner (1516–65) in his book *Concerning Fossils,
Rocks, and Crystals,* is formed through crystallization
in water. This idea would be adopted two centuries
later by Neptunists.

Johannes Kepler (1571–1630), the famous German
astronomer, gave his theory of volcanism: Just as the
human body produces tears and excrement, the earth
engenders amber, bitumen, sulfur, and underground
fires. His countryman, geographer Bernhard Varen
(1622–50), published a catalogue of the world's
volcanoes; twenty-seven were then known.

Italian philosopher Giordano Bruno (1548–1600),
noticing that many volcanoes were close to the sea,
concluded from this that volcanic activity must result
from the interaction between water and fire.

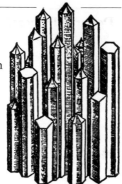

Believing that basalt columns crystallize in water, Konrad von Gesner depicted them (above) with pyramidal points like quartz crystals. He thought, wrongly, that these columns could not occur on active volcanoes like Etna (below, around 1550) but that they were confined to sedimentary regions.

Descartes Proposed a History of the Earth's Formation

The French mathematician and physicist René Descartes (1596–1650) made a major contribution to the scientific study of the origin and structure of the earth. He prudently began by affirming that his hypothesis was false and that of course the world was created in a single instant by God. He then explained that it was formed in three successive layers, which foreshadowed current studies of plate tectonics.

Gottfried von Leibniz (1646–1716), a German

A bove: Descartes saw the earth as a "cooled star," except at its center, where incandescent material survived. But he also imagined that the sun's rays had penetrated to the center of the earth and that the resulting heat broke the external crust. Certain sections straddle each other, while others have been raised above the water to form the continents.

philosopher and mathematician, adopted Descartes' views in principle but added the notions of magma and an incandescent globe that, since its birth, has cooled, contracted, and become folded on its surface.

In Kircher's Version, the Globe's Interior Is a Labyrinth

German Jesuit scholar Athanasius Kircher (1601–80) made his mark with an impressive work, *Underground World,* in which he largely espoused the ideas of Aristotle. However, he imagined that inside the globe there exist innumerable sources of fire (*pyrophylacia*), in fact reservoirs of magma, which communicate with the same number of "air vents": volcanoes. Noticing that the temperature increases as one descends into a mine, he thought about developing a machine for clearing out the chimneys of volcanoes to prevent them from erupting!

This engraving of Vesuvius (above), by Athanasius Kircher, shows a reservoir of magma in the bowels of the volcano.

At the End of the 17th Century, Chemistry Was Applied to the Functioning of Volcanoes

Englishmen Robert Hooke (1635–1703), a chemist and mathematician, and Martin Lister (c. 1638–1712), a doctor, claimed that, just as haystacks spontaneously combust through heat generated by decomposition, so underground fires are set off when pyrite and sulfur come into contact with air and the salt in seawater.

French pharmacist Nicolas Lémery (1645–1715) noticed that a mixture of iron filings and sulfur dampened with water heats up spontaneously to the point of incandescence, giving off violent emissions of steam accompanied by ejecta. He had just invented, he thought, a little artificial volcano.

Two eruptions marked the 17th century: In 1631 Vesuvius killed at least 4000 people in *torrens cineris*, torrents of ash, which today would be called pyroclastic flows; in 1669 Etna buried part of the town of Catania under lava. During this catastrophe people tried for the first time to divert a lava flow by cutting a hole in the banks— with a degree of success.

Kircher was one of the first people to draw the interior of the earth in any detail. He imagined it to be studded with interconnected pockets of fire. According to him, every eruption was a fire fanned by winds. It was hardly surprising that Aeolus, god of the wind, reigned in the Aeolian (Lipari) Islands, a string of volcanoes, two of which (Vulcano and Stromboli) are still active. Today volcanologists think that the deepest reservoirs of magma are only about 435 miles below sea level and that it is highly improbable that they are connected with the earth's core. Vesuvius' reservoir is thought to be 3 miles below, Etna's about 12 miles, and Stromboli's 150 miles.

The Beginnings of a Great Controversy

In 1707 the emergence of a new island in the middle of the Santorin caldera excited scholars. Basing his theory on observations of this event and on reports of the birth of Monte Nuovo in 1538, an Italian priest, Anton-Lazzaro Moro (1687–1740), explained that the action of volcanoes entails an uplift of the ground in the immediate vicinity. Thus, he maintained, all continents, islands, and mountains were born this way, and all stratified rocks are volcanic. As for the origin of underground fire, "God willed it."

By contrast, according to Benoît de Maillet (1656–1738), France's consul in Egypt under Louis XIV, all terrestrial rocks are marine deposits, and volcanic fire is a secondary phenomenon arising from the combustion of animal fats buried in sediments. (Fearing the anger of the Church for mocking the story of the Flood, he asked that his work be published ten years after his death.) These two explanations, radically opposed to each other, foreshadowed the great struggle of the 18th century: Plutonists versus Neptunists.

Moro's *Crustaceans and Other Marine Bodies Found in Mountains* (above) argued for the importance of volcanism in geological phenomena.

Catania was partially engulfed by Etna's lava on three occasions, the most recent in 1669 (opposite above). During Vesuvius' eruption of 1631 (opposite below) most of the valleys radiating down from the cone were swept by lethal ash flows.

Castell'Amare

F

D

due galere che andorno à pigliare li genti rimasti vivi.

Nomi de tutte le Torre e Ca abruggia
A. Portici
B. Pietra bi
C. Ririno
D. Torre de
ariceo

The 18th century, known as the Age of Enlightenment, was a decisive time in the history of volcanology. Slowly, by means of observation, scientists were able to improve on the ideas of the ancients. The scholars of this period traveled across Europe, collecting lava samples, comparing known volcanoes, and discovering new ones. Two opposing interpretations arose—and an epic, ruthless struggle began.

CHAPTER III
NEPTUNISTS VERSUS PLUTONISTS

Numerous artists have been fascinated by volcanoes. Some have painted them with great realism, like Saverio Della Gatta in this depiction of Vesuvius' eruption on 18 June 1794 (opposite). Others have been more fanciful—for example, the creator of this 1840 lithograph of Baron Munchausen, a German soldier and raconteur, being introduced to Vulcan and Venus (right).

This is how Comte Georges-Louis Leclerc de Buffon (1707–88), ironmaster, director of the Jardin du Roi (now the Jardin des Plantes) in Paris, learned naturalist, author of the 44-volume *Natural History,* (1749–1804), philosopher, and businessman, magnificently summarized how volcanoes were imagined in the mid-18th century: "A cannon of immense volume whose opening is often more than half a league across: This broad mouth of fire vomits torrents of smoke and flames, rivers of bitumen, sulfur, and molten metal, clouds of ash and stones.... There is...pyrite...which ferments every time it is exposed to air or humidity.... It catches fire, which causes an explosion in proportion to the quantity of inflamed material.... That is what a volcano is to a physicist."

He added that "the underground fires can act violently only when they are close enough to the sea that the great volume of water can produce enough force."

Water Feeds Volcanic Fires

This is, he thought, the explanation for the long dormant phases separating Etna's eruptions. If the volcano remained relatively calm in Homer's time

Above: Phases of an explosive eruption of the peak of Ternate, an island in the Moluccas of Indonesia.

French naturalist Buffon compared geologists to augurs, the official diviners of ancient Rome; he was represented in that guise in a contemporary print (below).

(c. 1000 BC), it was because the Mediterranean had withdrawn from the coasts of Sicily. When it became active again—from the time of Pindar (5th century BC) on—it was because the Strait of Gibraltar had broken through, allowing the sea to inundate the foot of Etna and feed it with water. Buffon proposed that dams should be built between the sea and volcanoes to prevent eruptions.

Buffon believed that the origins of volcanic activity are close to a volcano's summit, where great winds can maintain combustion. He cited the example of Ternate, in the Moluccas (Indonesia), which, according to a traveler's account, "is more inflamed and more furious in the periods of

The first documents reporting volcanic activity at La Fournaise on Réunion (formerly Bourbon, below) date from 1644. Since then, there have been more than 170 eruptions.

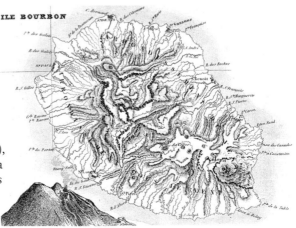

ILE BOURBON

equinoxes…because certain winds blow then which contribute to setting ablaze the material that vomits this fire." The Abbé de La Caille (1713–62) claimed that on the island of Bourbon (now Réunion), in the Indian Ocean, the volcano burned brighter during the cyclone season.

Buffon had never seen a volcano. He constructed his theory purely from the accounts of other scholars of the

The coat of arms of Guatemala City (left) is decorated with a chain of volcanoes. Three volcanoes are often active in Guatemala: Pacaya, Fuego, and Santa Maria, whose eruption in 1902 killed 6000 people.

Much of our information about eruptions comes from clergymen, such as Canon Recupero (opposite), who were both fascinated by hell and passionately interested in science.

period. Among these were Frenchmen Pierre Bouguer (1698–1758) and Charles-Marie de La Condamine (1701–74), who, while on a scientific expedition to South America in 1742, witnessed the eruption of Cotopaxi, in Ecuador, when the resulting mud flows engulfed hundreds of people and houses. When Cotopaxi heated up, the covering of ice on top of the volcano melted. Scholars therefore classed it among the "water volcanoes," like Agua in Guatemala, in contrast to the "fire volcanoes," such as Vesuvius.

JOSEPH CANONICUS RECUPERI

For descriptions of Vesuvius' behavior, Buffon relied especially on the priests Giuseppe Maria Mecatti and Giovanni Maria Della Torre, who both wrote accounts of eruptions, including imposing treatises on Vesuvius. Della Torre, who made minutely detailed observations, described the volcano's different types of flows and suggested that there could not be any fires under the earth because there was no air to maintain the combustion: This was a revolutionary idea.

For descriptions of Etna, Buffon drew from the fictional writings of the English traveler Patrick Brydone and the observations of Canon Giuseppe Recupero, author of the impressive *History of Etna*. These two men, who met in Sicily, compared the activities of Etna and Vesuvius. The stones ejected by Etna take twenty-one seconds to fall, said Recupero, and those of

"The last fire of Cotopaxi [left], that of 1742…caused no harm except through melting snow, although it opened a new mouth on the side, toward the center of the part that is continually under snow, while the flame still came out of the top of the truncated cone. There were two sudden floods: that of 24 June and that of 9 December; but the latter was incomparably greater…. The waves it formed in the countryside were over 60 feet high and in some places rose to more than 120…. They must have traveled 40 or 50 feet per second."
        Charles-Marie de La
        Condamine and
        Pierre Bouguer,
        The Form of the Earth,
        1749

Vesuvius touch ground after nine seconds, noted Brydone. From this they concluded that Etna is a much bigger volcano than Vesuvius. Etna's air is very electrified, observed Brydone, which explains why the vegetation at the foot of the volcano is so abundant and vigorous.

The Abbé Bertholon even went so far as to claim that electricity, composed of "tiny particles of fire," was the cause of volcanic eruptions, and that, to prevent them, one simply needed to plant big iron bars in the ground to relieve the earth of its charge—a kind of anti-eruption device.

Volcanoes in France

In 1749, when the first volume of Buffon's *Natural History* was published, nothing was known of the origin of France's Massif Central (a plateau area in the Auvergne and Dauphiné regions in the south center of the country). In 1717 Guillaume Rivière pointed out the presence, on a mountain summit some 150 miles to the south, of "a quantity of pumice stone which will float on water." Thirty years later chemist Gabriel François Venel announced that he had discovered remains of volcanic structures nearby. But the volcanoes of the Chaîne des Puys, mountains in the Auvergne region, were not yet considered to be more than heaps of mining

waste or gigantic furnaces from Roman forges.

It was Jean-Etienne Guettard (1715–86), a doctor, botanist, mineralogist, and curator of the Duc d'Orléans' natural history collection, who established their true origin. In 1746 Guettard drew up the first geological map of France. It was to complete this work that, in 1751, he traveled to central France accompanied by the botanist and diplomat Chrétien-Guillaume de Lamoignon de Malesherbes (1721–94). Guettard had never seen a volcano, but had examined lava from Vesuvius and Bourbon (Réunion) in the Duc d'Orléans' collection.

At Moulins he noticed a black, porous stone being used in building construction. He immediately recognized it as lava. The inhabitants told him that it came from the city of Volvic. The two scholars were very excited and proceeded north to Riom. Almost the whole town was built with this stone! They visited the nearby quarries of Volvic, followed the path left by a lava flow, and climbed a hill overlooking the village. Guettard

During Vesuvius' big eruptions—like that of 1779 (left) when a fountain of lava rose several thousand feet in the air—incessant flashes of static electricity make streaks in the plumes of ash, accompanied by alarming claps of thunder. Thunder and lightning are caused by the friction of lava particles and the ionized gases in the atmosphere. In 1631, several peasants were struck by lightning caused by the eruption. So it is not surprising that some 18th-century scholars proposed that volcanic activity had an electrical origin.

Below: A fountain made of lava at Moulins, France.

noted that the hill was comprised of materials ejected during volcanic eruptions and that there was a funnel-shaped crater at the top.

The next day he climbed the Puy de Dôme, the highest peak in the Chaîne des Puys. Noticing the layers of "burned materials," Guettard decided the mountain must be a volcano. From its peak he identified several more volcanic cones and then went further south in the Auvergne, where he immediately recognized remnants of other volcanic activity.

"It May Require Only the Slightest Movement and the Smallest Cause to Make Them Blaze Up Again"

In 1752 Guettard presented his famous memoir, *On Certain Mountains in France That Were Once Volcanoes*, to the Academy of Sciences in Paris. Not content with having discovered the volcanic origin of the Auvergne mountains, he also wrote in his account that they were probably only dormant. He even warned the inhabitants to watch out for signs foreshadowing an eruption, and, "on the occasion of earthquakes, to take the precautions that it is never shameful and always wise to take at such times."

A quarter of a century later, in 1778, Barthélemy Faujas de Saint-Fond (1741–1819), who was to hold the first chair in geology at Paris' natural history museum,

Faujas, depicted here (left) when he was Royal Commissioner of Mines, took a great interest in the pozzolana of the French volcanic cones and developed its use in cement. He was such a close friend of Buffon that the latter bequeathed to him his brain in an urn. The title page (opposite) and an engraving (background) from Faujas' book.

published in his magnificent *Researches into the Extinct Volcanoes of the Vivarais and the Velay* a letter sent to him by a man who had accompanied Guettard to the Puy de Dôme. This man claimed that, a year before, he had shown the site to the Irishman William Bowles (1703–80), who was on his way back from Vesuvius with an English colleague. He wrote, "It was then that I learned for the first time how to recognize craters and lava." So these two foreigners were shown to be the real "discoverers" of the Auvergne's volcanoes—a slap in the face for Guettard. It is true that he and Faujas disliked each other. Their enmity dated back to a journey they made to the Vivarais in 1775. Faujas, who had just established that this region is dotted with cones, flows, and "juices" of volcanic origin, feared that his colleague might steal his discovery. And Guettard did!

Water or Fire? The Origin of Basalt

Curiously, Guettard still mistakenly believed in the aqueous origin of basalt, claiming that it resulted from chemical precipitation in a marine environment. "If a columnar basalt can be produced by a volcano, why do we not find any among the recent eruptions of Vesuvius and other active volcanoes?" Faujas, on the other hand, thanks to his precise observations on the columnar basalt found in regions of France and Scotland, affirmed basalt's igneous and volcanic origin.

Guettard's discoveries and beliefs were—unknown to him—the foundations of two schools that were to clash violently for a long time. His ideas about basalt were to be adopted by the Neptunists (after Neptune, god of the sea), while his observations on the volcanoes of the Auvergne fed the ideas of the volcanists, or Plutonists (after Pluto, god of the underworld).

Abraham Gottlob Werner (1750–1817), the Great Master of Neptunism

A child prodigy in mineralogy, Werner was only twenty-six when he became professor at the Freiberg School of Mining, in Germany. He remained in this post for forty years. He published a classification of minerals, curiously entitled *On the Exterior Characteristics of Fossils,* which was a milestone in the field. Werner limited his field observations to the regions of Erzgebirge, Saxony, and Bohemia. He very quickly became an authority on "geognosy," the branch of geology dealing with

Werner (above), the "pope of Neptunism," was an unlikely supporter of a theory that said rocks originated by chemical precipitation: He lived in a region rich in extinct volcanoes and, as a young man, was inspector of the foundries of Saxony, where he could observe at leisure the volcanolike melting in the great furnaces.

the constitution of the earth. His clear and colorful style of teaching fascinated his numerous pupils, who came from all over Europe. He devoted all his time to them, even going so far as to lodge some of them in his own house. He hated writing—he did not even open his mail, for fear of having to answer it—and published only two small books and a few notes. Werner left to his disciples the task of spreading the good word and applying his principles and hypotheses around the world. When the Paris Academy of Sciences bestowed on him the title of foreign member, he did not even send his thanks. The French academicians forgave him, however, when they learned that a messenger sent to him by his sister in Dresden waited for two months at an inn (at Werner's expense) just for a signature for an urgent family matter.

His "geognosic" theory, which agreed perfectly

According to Werner, the basalt columns of Stolpen in Saxony (a 19th-century engraving, above) show no trace of melting. He thought their columnar nature was caused by desiccation, like cracks in drying mud.

A volcano and nearby section of geological formations (below).

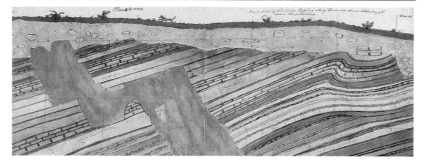

with the Book of Genesis in the Bible, proposed that the globe is cold inside and was long ago covered by a primitive ocean. On this basis nearly all rocks, including basalt, obsidian, pumice, and granite, were formed through chemical precipitation, crystallization, and sedimentation in the sea.

As for volcanoes, Werner believed they are unimportant recent accidents caused by coal fires that have melted nearby rocks into lava flows. This theory was based, no doubt, on Werner's observation that the volcanic hills of Bohemia are close to coal deposits.

The Opposing Plutonist School Was Led by a Scot, James Hutton (1726–97)

Doctor, chemist, and founder of a highly profitable ammonium chloride factory, Hutton took up agriculture to develop his land in Berwickshire, in southeast Scotland. It was while working in his fields that he discovered his interest in geology. He decided to devote himself henceforth to geological research and founded the Oyster Club, whose members—a few Edinburgh scholars—would gather every week to debate the great scientific problems of the day.

Hutton studied Castle Rock, Arthur's Seat, and Salisbury Crags—

Above: The section of terrain cut along a sewer under Frederick Street in Edinburgh shows an intrusion of basalt into sediments.

ancient volcanic features of Edinburgh. With no preconceptions, he first accumulated observations and then tried to explain them, in contrast to Werner, who preferred to impose his theories on the observed facts. In 1795, two years before his death, Hutton published his *Theory of the Earth,* which outlined the basis of Plutonism. Again in contrast to Hutton, he opposed the Book of Genesis, to the extent that he saw no start or end to the history of the world. The book is written in an obscure style and was to pass relatively unnoticed. A few years later mathematician John Playfair (1748–1819), in his *Illustration of the Huttonian Theory of the Earth*, set out his mentor's ideas in a clear, precise style that is a masterpiece of geological writing.

Volcanoes, said Hutton, communicate directly with the terrestrial core, which is molten for unknown reasons. In his view, the internal heat of the globe is periodically relieved by eruptions, causing great intrusions of molten materials into the earth's crust and upheavals of the ground. However, he remained convinced throughout his life that the outcroppings of volcanic rock in Scotland were set in place underground; he never imagined for a second that they poured out on the surface. As for sediments accumulating in water, he considered that they are consolidated and transformed into rocks by the action of internal heat during intrusions: the "metamorphism" of modern geology.

Hutton and an assistant examine sedimentary rocks covered by a layer of basalt, near Edinburgh (above).

Hutton (opposite) was irritated by religious beliefs about volcanism: "The volcano was not created to scare superstitious minds and plunge them into fits of piety and devotion. It should be considered as the vent of a furnace."

During one of his geological excursions, Hutton discovered veins of red granite crossing grayish schists (metamorphic crystalline rocks). This discovery confirmed the igneous origin of granite. Hutton was so exuberant that his companions thought he had detected a seam of gold or silver.

Hutton's Theory Was Threatened

The Irish mineralogist Richard Kirwan (1733–1812) fired the first shot by claiming that in northern Ireland he had discovered marine fossils in basalt. But Hutton demonstrated that this was merely a fossiliferous clay that had been baked on contact with lava.

An even more virulent attack came from Robert Jameson (1774–1854), a professor at Edinburgh University and a former pupil of Werner. He called the Plutonists' theories "monstrosities" and decreed that there were no remains of volcanoes in Scotland. He even created the Wernerian Natural History Society, which published only works favorable to Neptunism. But, little by little, Jameson was forced to retract his argument, even going so far as to include articles by Plutonists. He finally dissolved his society.

Nevertheless, until the end of his life Jameson continued to teach "Wernerian nonsense," as it was called by a member of one of his last audiences, English evolutionist Charles Darwin (1809–82).

The basalt columns of Fingal's Cave (above), on the island of Staffa, Scotland, resemble a church pipe organ.

The Discovery of German Volcanoes

One scholar before Hutton, German Rudolph Raspe (1737–94), had guessed the volcanic origin of the basalt prisms in Ireland and Scotland. He even tried to explain their form: If the basalts are prism-shaped, he said, it is because they were formed during submarine eruptions. Successively a librarian, mineralogist, spy, industrialist, and romantic poet, Raspe is also credited with the discovery of remains of volcanoes in Germany in 1769. Five years later Baron von Dietrich identified the Kaiserstuhl, a mountain group in the Rhine valley,

Below: The Giant's Causeway is a 50-million-year-old basalt flow in Ireland that once flooded a vast valley. On cooling very slowly, the deep interior of the flow contracted, forming a regular pattern of cracks that created columns with five to eight sides.

as volcanic. In 1785 the German volcanoes were the subject of the first scientific memoir by a Russian volcanologist, Prince Dmitri Galitzin (1738–1803). Raspe was, in fact, to achieve lasting fame for another reason. While in the service of the Prince of Hesse, he embezzled some of his employer's funds and then fled

Baron Munchausen, the hero of Raspe's novel, achieved a volcanologist's dream: He climbed down into Etna's crater to discuss the mechanism of eruptions with Vulcan.

to Britain, where he published a novel, *The Adventures of Baron Munchausen.*

Sir James Hall (1761–1832) Verifies Hutton's Theory in the Laboratory

Paradoxically, Hutton had attached little importance to laboratory experiments, although this is what ultimately brought supporting evidence for his theory. James Hall, a member of Hutton's Oyster Club, had heard that at Leith, in a glassworks, some glass had accidentally crystallized in a tank because the workers had let it cool too slowly. He took samples of the crystals and melted them again. Cooling them quickly, he obtained glass once more. Conversely, if the cooling was slow, the material recrystallized. He repeated the experiment with basalt, readily obtaining either glass or a crystalline, rock-like lava, depending on the speed of the cooling. So, he inferred, volcanic rocks are the result of cooling slowly after being melted.

During a journey to Vesuvius, observing the dikes that cut Monte Somma on the north and east sides, Hall noticed that the lava is glassy near the edges and crystalline in the center. He deduced quite correctly that molten rocks had penetrated fissures, that on the edges they had cooled quickly, vitrifying (converting to glass) on contact with the cold rock nearby, but had cooled and crystallized slowly in the center. A few years later, Scotsman George Watt, son of James Watt, inventor of the steam engine, was to succeed in creating artificial basalt columns in an oven.

The Eifel region of western Germany comprises ash cones, domes of viscous lava, and craters that were created in the last 500,000 years. The most recent eruptions in Germany took place here about 10,000 years ago. Above: A 1790 engraving of the area.

Monte Somma, a ridge on the side of Vesuvius, is furrowed with dikes (below).

It is by observing the materials ejected by active volcanoes, like Vesuvius, that scientists are able to explain the formation of extinct volcanoes. They have determined that basalt columns are not the result of crystallization in water but are of igneous origin, and that eruptions are not fires close to the earth's surface but come from a source deep in its core. These are victories won by the Plutonists.

CHAPTER IV
THE ERA OF THE FIRST VOLCANOLOGISTS

Though an acute observer of eruptions, Sir William Hamilton (right), one of the greatest volcanologists, refused to launch great theories. This drawing (opposite), illustrating the gradual growth of the summit cone of Vesuvius between 8 July and 29 October 1767, is from Hamilton's book *The Phlegraean Fields.*

Desmarest contributed an essay to the famous encyclopedia of Denis Diderot and Jean Le Rond D'Alembert, illustrated with engravings of the eruption of Vesuvius in 1754 (left) and views of the interior of the crater in repose and during eruption (opposite). His passion for rocks was almost fanatical. When he visited Rome, museum attendants hesitated to let him enter because he had a reputation for hammering off pieces of the finest ancient statues in order to discover the kind of rock they were made of.

Plutonist ideas had gained a lot of ground on the European continent before Hutton set out his theory in Scotland. The most famous precursor was French geologist Nicolas Desmarest (1725–1815). Although he came from a modest background, he rose to become, in 1788, inspector-general and director of France's royal factories. It was while on a visit to the Auvergne region in 1763 to inspect paper mills that he explored the Chaîne des Puys. There he was struck by what he

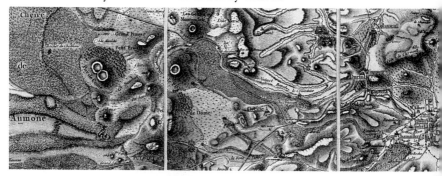

believed was abundant evidence that, contrary to accepted opinion, basalt and lava are not one and the same product of volcanic eruptions. In 1765 Desmarest presented his results to the French Academy of Sciences. His opinion was confirmed by other trips to the Auvergne and a visit to the

Above: Desmarest's map of the Chaîne des Puys, clearly showing craters and lava flows.

Italian volcanoes, naturally including Vesuvius. In 1771 he finally published his discovery as *Account of the Origin and Natures of the Great Polygonal Basalt Columns.* He then drew up the first geological map of the Chaîne des Puys and Mont-Dore, which was remarkably precise.

Desmarest Retraced the History of the Auvergne Volcanoes and Distinguished Three Epochs

The first epoch comprises volcanoes not long extinct, with flows that were still intact and covered with scoria (cindery lava). The volcanoes of the second epoch show flows modified by erosion, "the relief of the currents and valleys" having been inverted because of subsequent erosion by rivers—a phenomenon known today as inverted relief. Finally, the lava of the third epoch, the oldest, is layered between

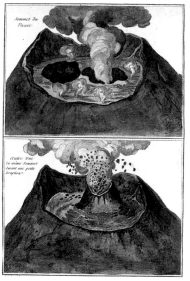

sedimentary rocks. The volcanoes of Limagne, near Clermont-Ferrand, made up of mixtures of sediments and lava fragments that have exploded on contact with water, are included in this group. Here again

B etween Clermont-Ferrand and Puy de Dôme, Desmarest noticed basalt columns that rested "on a bed of scoria and baked earth" and were covered by "a kind of foam which seems to have floated on the surface." He followed the columnar deposit and discovered that it was the product "of a flow emerging from a nearby volcano"—a revolutionary idea for the period.

L eft: The Puy de Pariou in the Chaîne des Puys.

Desmarest was putting forward an astonishingly accurate interpretation far ahead of anyone else.

There are only two significant errors in Desmarest's observations: First, he thought that basalt was derived from the melting of granite because he observed inclusions of this rock in lava; second, he thought that the Puy de Dôme was made up of granitic rocks that had melted in situ. Desmarest declared himself a Plutonist but never became involved in the quarrel with the Neptunists, instead telling them, "Go and see."

Scientific Explorations Increased, and New Volcanoes Were Studied

English explorer Captain James Cook (1728–79) visited Hawaii and its volcanoes in 1779, Frenchman Louis-Antoine de Bougainville (1729–1811) went around the world, and German Peter Pallas (1741–1811) explored Siberia.

A few years later, Jean Baptiste Geneviève Bory de Saint Vincent (1778–1846), a colonel, member of parliament, and fine naturalist, visited the Canary Islands—which he took to be the remains of Atlantis—and then went on to Réunion and the Cyclades. In his account, published in 1804, he gave a detailed description of Piton de la Fournaise on Réunion, whose summit crater was then being filled with molten lava. Nothing escaped his

ESSAIS

SUR

LES ISLES FORTUNÉES

ET L'ANTIQUE ATLANTIDE,

OU

PRÉCIS

DE l'Histoire générale de l'Archipel des Canaries,

PAR J. B. G. M. BORY DE ST.-VINCENT,

OFFICIER FRANÇAIS.

In 1801, when Bory visited the Piton de la Fournaise, the summit crater was occupied by a lake of molten lava; to the east a knoll (right) was formed by the accumulation of small flows of viscous lava above a vent.

eye: the different types of flow, the rocks with and without olivine (a greenish mineral), the lava tunnels, and even the threads of volcanic glass which, fifty years later on Hawaii, would be called "Pelé's hair." And he correctly explained all these phenomena. He baptized the principal craters of La Fournaise's peak, giving them the names of scholars: Faujas de Saint Fond, Dolomieu, and others, not forgetting to include himself, naming the summit crater Bory. Also during the late 18th and early 19th centuries—thanks to the work of a

Joseph Henri Hubert (1747–1825) was Bory's guide on Réunion and generously gave him all his observations on the activities of Piton de la Fournaise. This 1802 map of the volcano (which shows a lava flow reaching the sea) was largely inspired by Hubert's work.

number of scientists and observers all over the world —many false assumptions about volcanoes were laid to rest: Lava is not the result of fires raging underground; volcanoes are not vast, elevated furnaces lit on the shores of oceans to purge their waters of the oils caused by the decomposition of organic matter; and eruptions are not caused by the combustion of underground petroleum distilled through the fermentation of pyrite.

The Exciting Adventures of Déodat de Gratet de Dolomieu (1750–1801)

A geologist from the Dauphiné region of southeastern France, Knight of Malta, professor at the School of Mines in Paris, and member of the Academy of Sciences, Dolomieu was passionate about both volcanoes and women, explaining that "the study of stones does not extinguish one's sensitivity." He was to give his name to the Dolomite range in the Italian Alps, and to dolomite, the calcium magnesium carbonate rock of which they are composed.

Ground oscillations, probably caused by the presence of magma in an underground reservoir located 2 or 3 miles below the surface, took place around Pozzuoli, an ancient town near Naples. Displacements were greatest under the columns of the Roman marketplace and a temple: In the 10th century the ground sank about 19 feet; in 1538, when Monte Nuovo was born, the ground rose nearly 20 feet, then sank 13 feet after the eruption; between 1969 and 1984 it rose almost 12 feet.

Because of several tragic incidents during his life, he might easily have remained unknown. At the age of eighteen he was condemned to life imprisonment for having killed his opponent in a duel. Fortunately, he was pardoned. During the French Revolution nearly all his family died on the scaffold. His old friend and protector, the Duc de La Rochefoucauld, was murdered in his presence.

Dolomieu took part in Napoleon Bonaparte's expedition to Egypt in 1798, but on his return he was taken prisoner by counterrevolutionaries in Taranto, Italy, where his ship had run aground. For twenty-one months he was left imprisoned in Messina, in northwest Sicily. Desperate, ill, on the verge of suicide, he still found strength to write his will...and a classification of minerals. His most

Above: A map of the Bay of Naples and Vesuvius in 1793. Below: A drawing of Dolomieu, brilliant but unlucky.

influential friends, Sir Joseph Banks, president of the
Royal Society in London, Sir William Hamilton, and
Viscount Horatio Nelson, all tried, in vain, to get
Dolomieu released. The victory of the French in
1800 at Marengo, Italy, changed the situation:
Bonaparte demanded and obtained Dolomieu's
freedom. Dolomieu returned to France and
resumed his research, but he died a year later at
the age of fifty-one.

Dolomieu: A Founder of Modern Volcanology

Dolomieu saw active lava flows at Vesuvius and Etna,
and he saw Stromboli explode and Vulcano fuming; he
described these phenomena at length. He had no
doubts that the center of the earth was fluid—
composed of incandescent magma—and that lava
originated at a great depth. He said volcanic
activity was like that of a mole whose "works...
take place below the
lawn, putting soil
taken from a layer

During his visits to
the Auvergne,
Vesuvius, and the Lipari
Islands, Dolomieu
assembled a vast
collection of volcanic
rocks and minerals. In
the basalts of the
Cyclades he even
discovered a new mineral,
analcime. Below: An
18th-century engraving
of the interior of
Etna's crater.

just below onto the surface."

While his predecessors saw molten granite as the source of all lava, Dolomieu claimed that the diversity of lava types comes from the fact that each originates in a special type of rock located beneath the earth's crust. He differentiated the black basalts from whitish felsite and understood that the pumice of Lipari Island was merely obsidian saturated with gas bubbles. But he was mistaken in his claims that lava flows because of a combustion of sulfur and that the big black crystals scattered throughout the flows of Etna and Vesuvius are the unmelted remains of rocks from deep in

In his prison at Messina, the only paper Dolomieu had to write on were the blank areas and margins of Faujas de Saint Fond's *Mineralogy of Volcanoes.*

"I ask the person into whose hands this book may fall.... I beg them by everything they may hold dear, to deliver it in France to my sister Alexandrine.... I beg my dear sister to give ten golden louis to the person who will deliver this book to her, which is the last testament of my love for her."

Déodat de Gratet de Dolomieu

the earth where the lava originates. In an area near Etna, Dolomieu detected the submarine origin of the basalts.

At Vesuvius, which Dolomieu visited with Sir William Hamilton and James Hall, he noticed the presence of "vertical lava" in Monte Somma. This, he said, was lava that had flowed from the top to the bottom in open fractures: We now know this to be wrong. The pillars of lava are, in fact, dikes—that is, fissures filled with cooled magma that has come up from the depths.

Being an ardent volcanologist, Dolomieu decided to visit the Auvergne, too. He proposed raising money to pay for boring into the granite beneath a volcanic cone to reach the volcano's source! He claimed that the basalt columns of France's Massif Central were formed by the contraction of lava as it cooled. He correctly explained that the Puy de Dôme "came out of the earth like a sort of swelling lifted up by volcanic activity…and must have been in a viscous state to retain its form as it rose." And he maintained that the bituminous hills in that region—presented by many as proof of underground fires—were "not connected with volcanoes except by being in their vicinity."

The Volcanological Ambassador

One of Dolomieu's friends made a great contribution to his Plutonist ideas. Sir William Hamilton, the English ambassador to the court of Naples and husband of the notorious English beauty Emma Hart, was an excellent dancer, musician, and archaeologist, but he was especially a volcanologist with a passion for Vesuvius: He climbed it more than sixty times—even during eruptions—risking his own life and that of his guide.

In his letters to the Royal Society in London, as well as in several of his works, including the renowned *The Phlegraean Fields,* with its hand-colored engravings, Hamilton gave admirable descriptions of the eruptions of Vesuvius from 1766 to 1794, as well as of the Phlegraean Fields, the summit of Etna, the Lipari Islands, and even the volcanoes along the Rhine, in Germany. His writings were to have a tremendous effect throughout Europe.

Hamilton witnessed the eruption of Vesuvius in 1779, when the fountain of lava reached an impressive height (opposite, above), and that of 1794, when lava destroyed Torre del Greco (opposite below, in a contemporary plan and elevation). He compared Vesuvius (above, in 1756) to a "body full of bad humors" which are evacuated through the volcano's summit crater. But if these humors are obstructed, the body is shaken with earthquakes, and the humors then seek another exit.

Hamilton tried to date the ancient lava flows of Vesuvius by means of their plant cover, and noted that, although piled up on top of each other, the layers of lava were often separated by deposits of soil whose thickness corresponded to the length of the period of repose between flows. He collected thousands of volcanic rocks, as well as sublimates from the Solfatara (opposite below), to have them analyzed in London. At Pompeii he was present at the excavation and exhumation of many of those who died, asphyxiated and crushed beneath the falls of pumice (opposite above). He noticed that by means of the size and weight distribution of pumice stones one can discover the place from which they were ejected. He was the first to announce that the volcano that annihilated Pompeii and Herculaneum in AD 79 was actually not Vesuvius but the curved volcanic ridge that encircles it to the north: Monte Somma. The present cone of Vesuvius was formed afterward, in the gutted crater of its predecessor (left, when active in 1779).

Hamilton Understood that Volcanic Power Is an Essential Phenomenon of Planet Earth

Hamilton was lucky enough to observe the eruptions of Vesuvius while they were happening. He established once and for all that the source of volcanoes is not near the surface, as Buffon had claimed, but deep inside the earth. In Hamilton's view, volcanic heat is of a special kind, since eruptions even take place underwater, where there is no air to maintain combustion. He rightly claimed that volcanic cones grow through the accumulation of layers of ash and lava.

Hamilton differentiated two types of lava: that which resembles "petrified cables" (ropy lava) and that which he described as being like the Thames in winter, when the river melts and carries off slabs of snow and blocks of ice (slaggy or scoriaceous lava). His observations of quarries dug in hardened flows showed that lava can be slaggy at the base and the top but massive and sometimes prismatic in the middle. He noted the presence of basalt columns on an active volcano and concluded correctly that wherever such formations exist there has been volcanic activity. Hamilton even hit on the modern explanation for the explosive phases of Vesuvius, characterized by great plumes of ash: These

In a volcanic grotto near Naples, guides carried out an experiment: When a dog was sent in, it was immediately asphyxiated by the carbonic gas inside; on being plunged into the lake, however, it would revive at once.

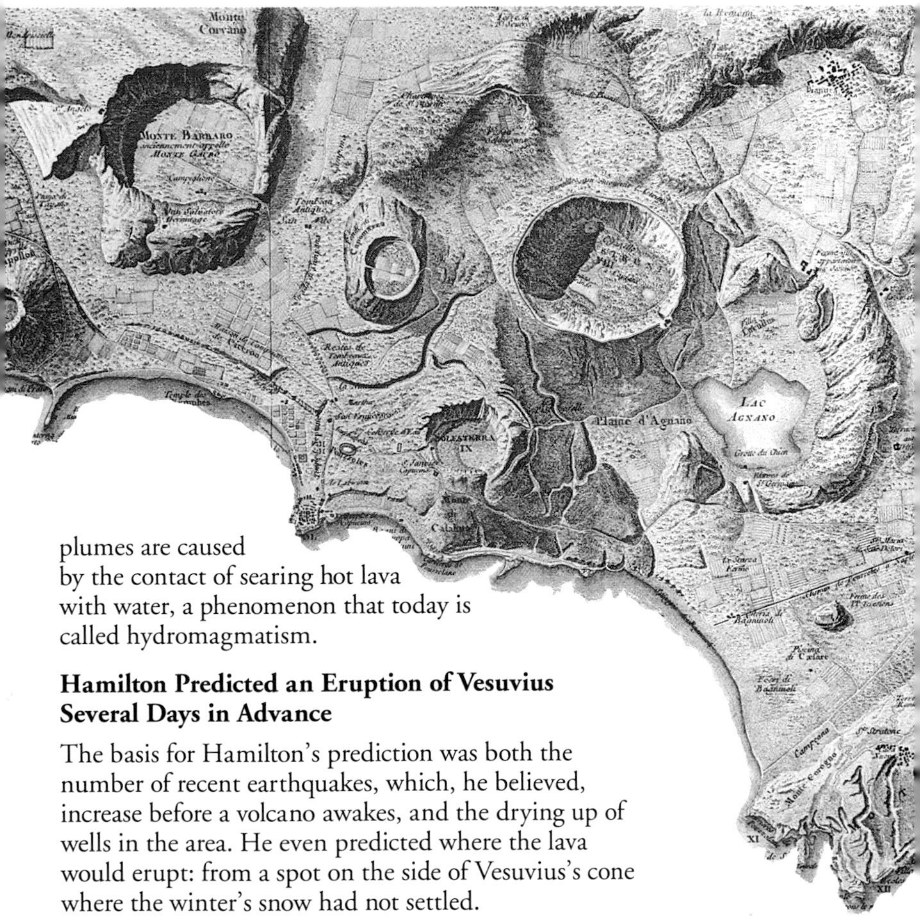

plumes are caused
by the contact of searing hot lava
with water, a phenomenon that today is
called hydromagmatism.

Hamilton Predicted an Eruption of Vesuvius Several Days in Advance

The basis for Hamilton's prediction was both the
number of recent earthquakes, which, he believed,
increase before a volcano awakes, and the drying up of
wells in the area. He even predicted where the lava
would erupt: from a spot on the side of Vesuvius's cone
where the winter's snow had not settled.

Being well acquainted with the risks that volcanoes
pose to people and property, Hamilton advised the king
and his court to leave the palace of Portici in a hurry,
because it was under threat from lava flows; he even
proposed that the flows be diverted. He also stressed
the dangers to cattle of the volcanic dust that would
spread over pastures, and the dangers of the fumarole
gases, hot toxic vapors that can kill through
asphyxiation. When the ashes fell on the roofs of

Above: The
Phlegraean Fields,
west of Naples, are
composed of 150
eruptive centers located
in an enormous caldera
(over 9 miles in diameter)
created 35,000 years ago
during a cataclysm that
ejected more than 24
cubic miles of ash.

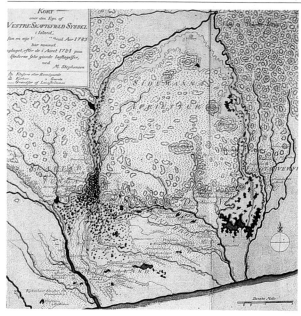

Naples, he insisted that they be cleaned off immediately to prevent the roofs' collapsing.

Another volcanologist, an Italian contemporary of Hamilton, took a passionate interest in the eruptive mechanisms of Italy's volcanoes. This was Lazzaro Spallanzani (1729–99), who was already known for his research on the circulation of the blood. He applied the same experimental method to volcanic rocks, extracting the gases they contain by melting them down. In this way he proved that, contrary to Dolomieu's opinion, the presence of sulfur in lava does not help it to melt.

In 1783 Eruptions Ravaged Iceland and Japan

The enormous outpouring of basalt at Laki, in southern Iceland—almost 3 cubic miles—was the biggest on record. It also spewed out more than 500 million tons of noxious gases; 11,000 cattle, 28,000 horses, and 200,000 sheep perished because of the contamination of their pastures and waters. A quarter

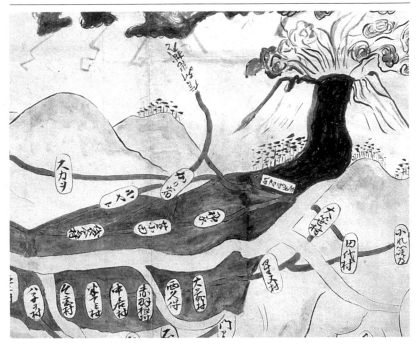

of Iceland's population, around 10,500 people, died in the resulting famine.

The winter of 1783–4 was terribly severe throughout Europe and North America, the ground remaining frozen until the start of summer. But Iceland was far away, and no volcanologist of the period was to refer to the eruption of Laki. Fortunately, the pastor Jón Steingrimsson, who lived close to where the cataclysm occurred, left a full description of it. The same year, in Japan, the sudden awakening of Asama, on the island of Honshu, killed almost 1200 people.

The Last Twitches of Neptunism

Ironically, it was the most brilliant pupils of Werner, the founder of this theory, who were to dig its grave. Having been trained at the Freiberg School of Mining, they tried to apply his model to the geology of the

Above: A drawing showing the area devastated by the ash, mud, and lava from Asama, Japan, in 1783. Asama is also shown on the following pages.

The eruptive fissure crowned with 135 craters (opposite left and detail opposite right) that opened during the eruption of Laki (Iceland) in 1783 was almost 16 miles long with flows of up to 40 miles in length.

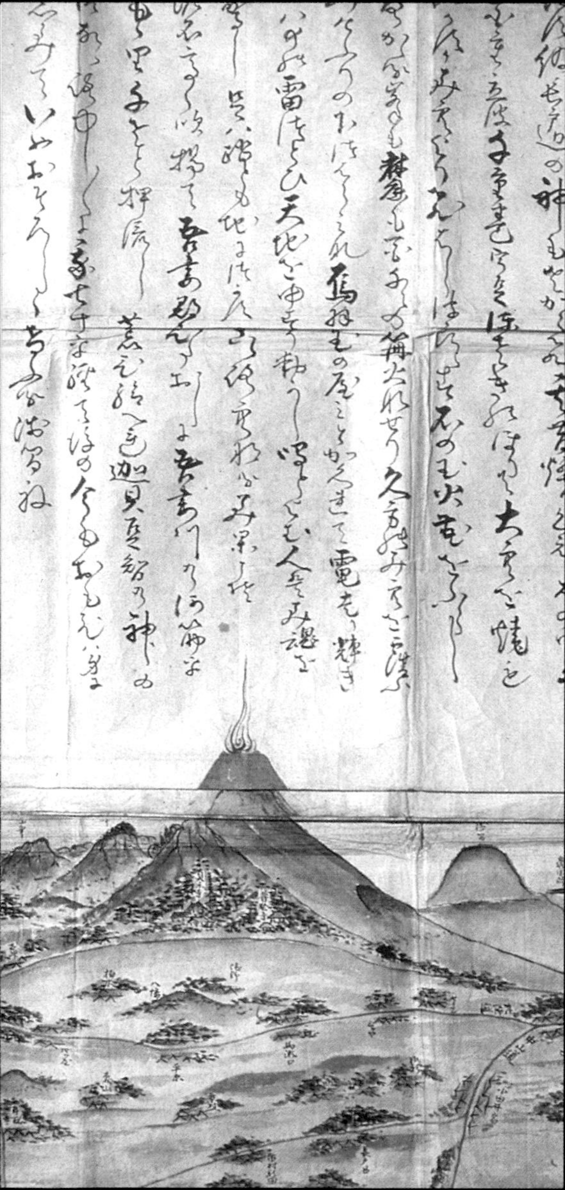

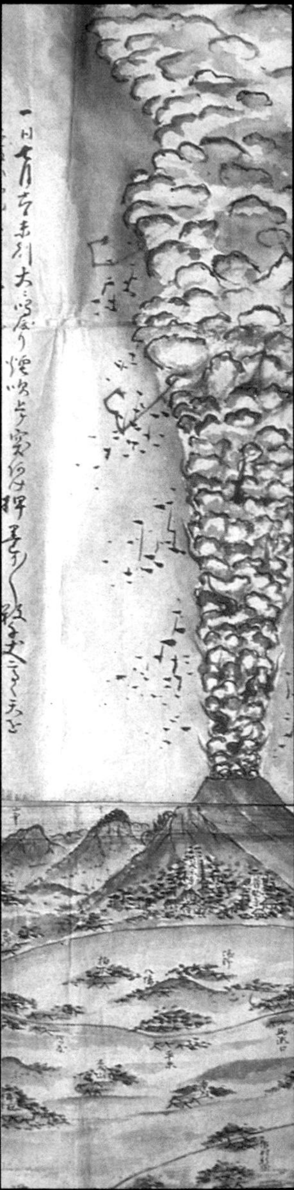

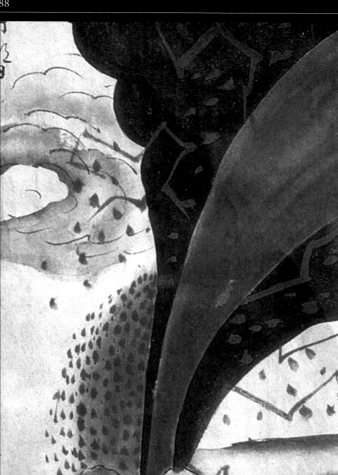

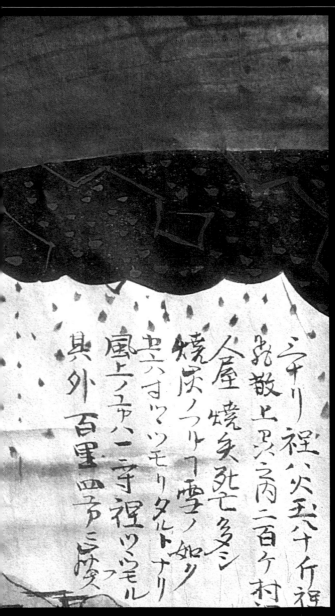

The Eruption of Asama

L eft and previous pages: Explosions of ash and pumice shook the summit. The rhythm accelerated, and by the end of July 1783 activity was continuous. On 4 August, 3.5 billion cubic feet of ash and molten scoria overflowed from the crater and slowly slid down the north side of the volcano, devastating almost 4500 acres. The next day a gigantic explosion was heard almost 200 miles away. A terrifying plume of ash streaked with lightning rose slowly and threw out enormous quantities of lava blocks—glowing red, sometimes more than 100 feet in diameter. These fell on the northern lip of Asama and were transformed into an avalanche of 350 million cubic feet, at more than 300° C, which rushed down the cone's very steep slope and swept aside four villages. On reaching the Agatsuma river, the avalanche unleashed a flood of muddy water that carried off 1200 houses. To end the cycle, a flow of 6 billion cubic feet of viscous lava descended the northern side for more than 3 miles before coming to a stop. The cataclysm claimed at least 1200 lives.

whole world, from Italy to Siberia, from Mexico to the Andean cordillera. They were to go from surprise to surprise, as, for example, in the case of the French scholar Jean François d'Aubuisson de Voisins (1769–1819). An ardent Neptunist, he had written a treatise on the basalts of Saxony, which he declared to be of aqueous origin. Then one day, in the Massif Central, he was studying the lava flows of the extinct volcanoes and was shocked to find that in several places they were composed of basalt. He had to recognize that "in the Auvergne one finds basalts of volcanic origin." He was forced to apply this conclusion to the basalts of Saxony.

Alexander von Humboldt (1769–1859) was to follow the same path. Astronomer, geophysicist, geologist, ethnographer, and diplomat, this great German explorer was also a pupil of Werner. His early work on the Rhine basalts was a model of Neptunism. But by 1794, when he described the craters of the Eifel region in Germany, doubt was creeping in.

Humboldt Traveled to Seek the Truth

In 1799 he set sail for the Americas. In five years he was to travel 6200 miles through the forests of the Orinoco and to the volcanoes of the Andes and Mexico. He climbed Puracé (Colombia, 15,604 feet), which spat out jets of steam with an appalling din, and Pichincha (Ecuador, 15,703 feet), which burned with bluish flames. Here, strong seismic tremors spread consternation through the population of Quito, who accused the scholar of being a heretic and of having provoked the shocks by throwing gunpowder into the crater. An excellent mountaineer, Humboldt reached the summit of

The watercolor opposite, taken from one of the volumes of his *Voyage of Humboldt and Bonpland*, shows Humboldt (also below) and members of his expedition arriving at the foot of Cayambe (18,996 feet), in northern Ecuador. Humboldt's literary output was tremendous. He first published the twenty-three volumes of *Voyage*, written between 1805 and 1834, in which he recorded all his research done in the Americas. Then for twenty-five years he devoted himself to the publication of the five-volume *Cosmos*, a description of the physical universe, but he died at the age of ninety, before it was finished.

Chimborazo (Ecuador, 20,561 feet), then the highest
point conquered by a human being. In Mexico he
made a detailed description of Jorullo, a new volcano
that had appeared in 1759, its lava flow studded with
thousands of little cones that were still smoking. On his
return from this triumphant expedition, accompanied
by his friends Simon Bolívar (1783–1830), Joseph-
Louis Gay-Lussac (1778–1850), and Baron Leopold
von Buch (1774–1853, also a student of Werner), he
observed Vesuvius as it erupted.

Humboldt was to divide the rest of his life between
Paris, which he adored, and Berlin, which he hated—
comparing its Academy of Sciences to a leper hospital
where it was impossible to tell the sick from the
healthy, after one of its members declared that
the Egyptian pyramids were volcanic cones.

An Original Approach to Volcanism, Mostly Concerning the Volcanoes of the New World

Humboldt expressed several concepts that still have
value today. Considering the distribution of volcanoes
on the surface of the planet, he noted that they
form long volcanic chains located on deep geological
faults, where the earth's crust is unstable. According
to him, volcanoes communicate with each other,
at least within their own regions. Thus, on the
high plateau of Quito, Pichincha, Cotopaxi, and
Tungurahua form "a single magmatic source." The
"underground fire erupts sometimes from one of these
openings, and sometimes from another...." Very high
volcanoes have fewer eruptions than those of low
altitude, because it is more difficult for lava to ascend
to their peaks.

He claimed that great destructive earthquakes have
no direct connection with volcanic activities, which
are the cause only of small local shocks—the precursor
of the present-day distinction between devastating
tectonic earthquakes and minor volcanic shocks.
Finally, according to Humboldt—though the idea was
already current—lava is not the product of combustion

On 29 September 1759, a new volcano, Jorullo (near left), was born in Mexico. The volcanic emissions exploded on contact with water and formed small cones resembling "bakers' ovens," according to Humboldt, who visited the area in 1803. Far left: Humboldt compared the height of Chimborazo (Ecuador's highest volcano, also depicted above) to Cotopaxi (Ecuador), Popocatépetl (Mexico), Mont Blanc (France), and the Pico de Teide (Tenerife, Canary Islands).

but a "fluid mixture of metals, alkalis, and earth" which rise to the surface because of "the expansion of steam." Humboldt the Neptunist had become a fervent Plutonist.

Baron Leopold von Buch, Werner's Favorite Pupil, Also Changed Sides

To avoid offending his mentor, Buch declared himself a Plutonist only after Werner's death. Born to a rich and noble family, Buch was unsociable and very shy but rapidly became the best-known geologist of the early 19th century. In the mines where he worked, contrary to Werner's theory, he found many basalts far from any coal source that might conceivably have caught fire and melted the rocks.

In 1797 Buch abandoned his duties at the mines to travel and devote himself to his private research. Two

Since 1700 the town of Torre del Greco, at the foot of Vesuvius, has been invaded three times by lava flows (1737, 1794, and 1805–6). The last eruption (pictured above) was observed by Buch.

years later he left for Italy on foot, taking with him only a silk shirt and silk socks, a notebook, his barometer, and a hammer. He first studied the Alban Hills, near Rome, where he became "lost in contradictions" over the origin of the basalts of Capo di Bove. Werner's ideas were not applicable here. Then he examined Vesuvius, which he called his "sublime mountain." He returned in 1805 to see it erupt. But here too, there was not a trace of coal.

Having decided to seek a better understanding of volcanism, he went, again on foot, to the Auvergne, where the beauty of the Puy de Pariou and the Puy de Dôme charmed him: "Do you wish to see volcanoes? Choose Clermont in preference to Vesuvius and Etna." Buch was quickly convinced that France's basalts were volcanic, but he maintained that those of Germany were certainly of aqueous origin, as he had learned from Werner.

A long sojourn in the Canary Islands and a visit to Scotland and northern Ireland proved to him that, contrary to Werner's opinion, volcanism is a major phenomenon of the planet and that the source of volcanoes lies in the depths of the earth. Tirelessly, he scoured Europe for volcanic sites. Throughout the rest of his life he continued to accumulate thousands of observations that would be the death knell for Werner's theories— Hutton had finally triumphed.

Curiously, Buch (below) was far more impressed by the basalt columns (above) and cones of the Massif Central than by the Italian volcanoes. He considered the Puy de Pariou to be a model volcano.

How does a volcano grow—by inflating, or through the accumulation of ash and lava? This was the final conflict between volcanologists. Once it was resolved, volcanology really took off. Research began to be conducted at sites of volcanic activity— present and past—all over the world. The study of gases, rocks, and the physics of the earth became widespread.

CHAPTER V
TOWARD MODERN VOLCANOLOGY

Since the prediction of eruptions is still in its infancy, the evacuation of nearby populations (as shown opposite in Galunggung, Java, in April 1982) is always a wise measure. To gain a better understanding of volcanism, scientists build model volcanoes (right).

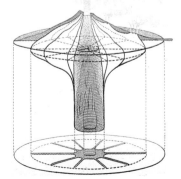

As the quarrel between Neptunists and Plutonists was dying down, another controversial idea was unleashing new passions: Leopold von Buch's theory of "uplifted craters." He developed his premise in the Massif Central and published it in 1842. Buch explained that dome-shaped volcanoes, like the Puy de Dôme, Sarcoui, and Puy Chopine, are made up of "granite changed and thrust upward" by underground steam. Conversely, the *puys* (peaks)

In this profile of the north of the Chaîne des Puys, drawn by Buch, the Puy de Dôme, Sarcoui, and Chopine, three domes of viscous lava, are depicted as outgrowths of the granite base.

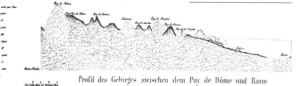

Profil des Gebirges zwischen dem Puy de Dôme und Riom

with craters formed of loose scoria were constructed through the accumulation of lava during explosions. He added, wrongly, that granite changes into "domite" (a name he made up), and that as this melts it produces basalt. A great step…backward.

Buch Saw the Puy de Dôme as a "Blister," or a "Balloon," That Rose Through "an Interior Volcanic Force"

Mountains thrust upward in this way would end by exploding, their rounded summit collapsing to create a circular "uplifted" crater with vertical walls, called a

George Poulett Scrope's *Memoir on the Geology & Volcanic Formations of Central France*, published in 1827, contains splendid panoramic views drawn by the author. Below: The south of the Chaîne des Puys, seen from the summit of the Puy de Rodde.

Between the 5th and 8th centuries, "domite" was quarried from the dome of Sarcoui (in blue) to make stone coffins. This earned it the nickname Mountain of Sarcophagi.

caldera. Buch differentiated between activity that raises and creates uplifted craters and that which produces eruption craters (*puys*).

Buch applied his theory to many other volcanic massifs, including Mont-Dore and Cantal in the Auvergne, which he correctly considered to be enormous masses that had been thrust upward and had then collapsed at their center. Vesuvius, he thought, had "emerged ready-made from the bosom of the earth," being in no way formed by the accumulation of lava flows. He even maintained, in

The ninety volcanoes of the Chaîne des Puys, the youngest in France (they were formed in the last 90,000 years), extend over almost 30 miles.

the face of all the evidence, that this volcano had never erupted pumice.

The Theory of Uplifted Craters Was a Huge Success

Humboldt was enthusiastic and wrote, wrongly, that during the eruption of Jorullo, in Mexico, "a plain of 3000 or 4000 square meters…rose like a balloon to a height of 160 meters…. Thousands of little cones, two or three meters high, emerged all over the place, in the middle of this domed plain…."

In France, two geologists, Armand Dufrénoy (1792–1857) and Elie de Beaumont (1798–1874), tried by every possible means to prove the hypothesis of uplifted craters. They applied their reasoning to Mont-Dore, Cantal, Vesuvius, and Etna, which they visited with Buch. The great, thick lava flows can only spread over almost flat surfaces, they explained. On slopes greater than 6°, lava can no longer maintain itself as a mass but fragments, losing its ability to spread. However, in the walls of many volcanic structures, the flows are inclined at more than 30°. So, they thought, volcanoes could have risen only after the accumulation of the great flows, which must have spread almost horizontally.

Dufrénoy, who tried to apply this theory to Vesuvius and the Phlegraean Fields, thought he had found a decisive argument when he discovered seashells on Monte Somma: He thought these shells must have been lifted with the volcano when it emerged from the sea. In fact, these are blocks of limestone embedded with shells that were torn from the volcano's substratum

when the magma rose. He also maintained that Monte Nuovo emerged from the earth in the shape of a vast blister which burst in such a way as to produce a crater.

De Beaumont claimed that Etna grew mainly through sudden and successive uplifts centered on the depression of the Valle del Bove, a valley that cuts into the mountain's eastern flank; he said that the emission of lava was merely "what is most striking to the eye." The uplifting had preceded the

E lie de Beaumont's map of Etna (left), published in 1838, shows the summit area, the Valle del Bove, and many smaller cones.

I n his *Physical Description of the Canary Islands* Buch wrote that the barrancos (deep gullies) radiating down the flanks of the volcano on the island of La Palma (prominent in Buch's 1814 engraving below) are fissures that opened during the upthrust. In fact they are ravines caused by erosion.

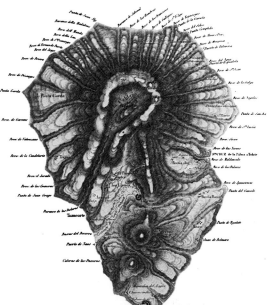

eruption. He was right at least about this last point, as the measurements of volcanic deformations carried out a century later would confirm.

In 1815 an enormous eruption decapitated Tambora, a volcano in Sumbawa, Indonesia, killing 10,000 people instantly and 82,000 others by the resulting famine. Sir Thomas Stamford Raffles (1781–1826), the English lieutenant governor of Java at the time, described the cataclysm and its climatic effects. But his observations passed almost unnoticed in Europe, where volcanologists were preoccupied with the controversy that was raging.

Buch's Theory Had No Shortage of Detractors. They Ferociously Resisted the Master's "Aberrations"

Buch's most virulent opponent was George Julius Poulett Scrope (1797–1876), an English politician and economist involved in the struggle against rural poverty but whose real vocation was volcanology. At the age of twenty he went to Italy. He climbed Etna, visited the Lipari Islands, and five years later, in 1822, witnessed a major eruption of Vesuvius.

Scrope was not yet thirty when he published his *Considerations on Volcanoes* (1825), in which he set out the basis of modern volcanology. He studied at length

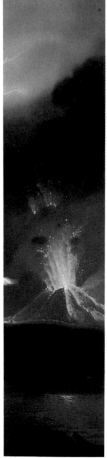

the accumulation of layers of ash and lava that built volcanic cones and proved that thick flows could spread evenly on slopes of more than 30°, thus casting serious doubt on Buch's theory of uplifted craters. Scrope's main contribution, however, was showing the

In 1821 English volcanologist Scrope (left) came to conclusions radically different from those proposed by French naturalists.

importance of the gases and water contained in the magma deep underground, which is under pressure from the weight of rocks on top of it. At the slightest drop in pressure, the gases separate from the solid, water is changed to steam—provoking the rise of molten material—and an eruption follows. He also noticed that when a volcano emits a succession of several different types of lava (for example, basaltic

The eruption of Vesuvius in 1822, seen by night (opposite) and by day (above). The plume rose to 6500 feet, and ashes fell over 100 miles away. A volcanic bomb of several tons was found in a garden about 3 miles from the crater.

followed by trachytic), it is because chemical processes have slowly modified the composition of the magma in the reservoir. As for the fluidity of lava, that depends on its mineralogical composition, its gas content, and its temperature. This was already a big step toward modern volcanology.

Scrope opposed the ideas of other physicists, who claimed that the heat of the earth was caused either by the weight of the rocks and by friction at great depths or by the interaction between percolating water and salts of calcium and sodium. Scrope believed, conversely, that the magma of the depths resulted from the heat that was created at the birth of our planet.

According to Scrope, the formation of the Chaîne des Puys was very recent, but earlier than Julius Caesar (100–44 BC), since no eruptions are mentioned in the contemporary texts describing his exploits in that area. Scrope pointed out the presence of carbonized wood at Saint-Saturnin, north of Clermont-Ferrand, under a layer of lava that originated in the Puy de la Vache and the Puy de Lassolas. A century and a half later these pieces of wood would help to provide the first radioactive dating of a flow in the Chaîne des Puys: They are 7600 years old.

Scrope Found an Important Ally in Sir Charles Lyell (1797–1875)

This British geologist, author of *The Principles of Geology* (the first modern book on the earth sciences), had read Scrope's work. He decided to travel to the Auvergne and Italy to investigate the subject further.

In the Massif Central everything Lyell saw confirmed Scrope's opinions. Lyell climbed Vesuvius, studied Ischia (an island in the Bay of Naples), and found marine mollusks there, at an altitude of 2900 feet. This

Charles Lyell (below) claimed that the geological phenomena of the past happened extremely slowly, just as the Egyptian pyramids were not built in a day.

phenomenon, he correctly explained, was the result of the uplifting of the volcanic island. Then he went to Etna, which he examined thoroughly. He returned there several times to explore the Valle del Bove.

Lyell described its dikes and the piling up of thick lava flows which had obviously spread on very steep slopes (up to 45°). He saw no evidence for an uplifted crater, as Elie de Beaumont had argued. Certainly, he said, the volcano had been uplifted—as proved by the marine sediments left high and dry, intercalated between the lava flows at Etna's base—but this uplifting did not happen suddenly, as Buch's disciples claimed, but very slowly and gradually.

Lyell's description of Etna, the morphology of its flows, and its parasitic cones is a masterpiece of precision. It was based on his own research as well as on that of a group of Sicilian naturalists, including the Gemmellaro brothers, who published an astonishing volcanological map of Etna in 1824 and described all its

Above: The 1819 eruption of Etna and the flow of lava through the Valle del Bove.

This volcanological map of Etna, drawn by Mario Gemmellaro in 1823 (below), shows all the volcano's historical flows, the parasitic cones, and the villages with the number of their inhabitants at the time.

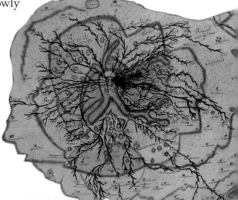

activities between 1803 and 1865.

In the same period German Baron
Wolfgang Sartorius von Waltershausen
(1809–76) drew up the detailed geological
maps of Etna's massif, which he published in
the form of an atlas in 1845, as well as two
fat explanatory volumes that appeared after
his death. Etna finally became, with
Vesuvius, one of the two most studied
volcanoes in the world.

In 1831 the Birth of a Volcano in the Sea Between Sicily and North Africa Nullified the "Uplifted Craters" Theory

This event rocked the political world. Some feared that
a chain of mountains would appear, linking Sicily to
Tunisia and disrupting the geopolitics of the whole
Mediterranean basin. The Sicilian government sent
representatives on the warship *Etna* to baptize the

On 13 July 1831,
when a volcano
sprang up between Sicily
and Tunisia, fountains of
lava gushed forth along a
fissure (above). The lava
exploded on contact with
seawater, spitting out so-
called cypress-shaped
clouds of black ash (top).

new islet Ferdinandea, in honor of its king, Ferdinand II (ruled 1830–59). At the same time, officers of the English fleet rushed to name it Graham. Finally, Constant Prévost (1787–1856), one of the founders of the French Geological Society, was dispatched to the scene by the Paris Academy of Sciences. He called the island Julia because the volcano was born in July. In his report to the Geological Society he affirmed that nothing in the formation of Julia resembled the swelling of an "uplifted crater," and that it rose only through accumulation. Using an image that was destined for a long life, he compared the eruption to a bottle of champagne being uncorked.

When Prévost arrived at the island, the volcano—230 feet high and 2300 feet in diameter—was still erupting (left). He disembarked, studied the rocks, and noted that the ash layers had a cross-bedded structure (they were caused by horizontal blasts, nowadays called base surges). He planted the French flag in the ground. As the English had also planted their own flag (above), a diplomatic incident ensued. The volcano solved the problem by disappearing on 28 December 1831, five months after its birth.

The theory of uplifted craters was further collapsed when Charles Lyell, accompanied by Georg Hartung, visited the Canary Islands. The two men understood that the calderas of Gran Canaria and La Palma were not caused by uplifting but by collapses and erosion, like those of Madeira and the Azores, which Hartung had studied.

The final blow was struck by Ferdinand-André Fouqué (1828–1904), a professor of petrography at the Collège de France, who in 1866 was sent to Santorin to study its caldera and the eruption that had just occurred. Santorin was considered by Elie de Beaumont and French chemist Henri Sainte-Claire Deville (1818–81) to be one of the finest examples of a sudden enormous uplifting.

Fouqué made a detailed study of the stratigraphy of the caldera's wall. Under a layer of pumice 90 to 100 feet thick, he discovered archaeological remains dating from 2000 BC. Here was proof of the island's collapse after an enormous, explosive eruption. "The theory of uplifted craters," he said, "must be abandoned definitively; it can henceforth be considered only as one of those noble wrecks that litter the path of science."

Following his voyage to observe Santorin's 1866 eruption (left), Fouqué published a study of the island. In it he described the growth of domes of viscous lava on Nea Kameni (below, shown between 11 February 1866 and 26 September 1867) and deduced that it was the viscosity of the magma that determined the shape of the volcanic structures. He also concluded, from the presence of two kinds of feldspar crystals in the lava, that there had been a mixing of magma in the depths of the earth. This idea would be adopted later by other volcanologists.

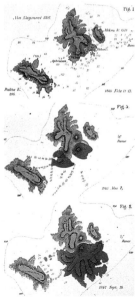

In a Mere Half Century, the Study of Gases Passed from Prehistory to the Modern Age

In 1822 the English chemist Sir Humphry Davy (1778–1829), who believed erroneously that volcanic heat came from the oxidation of alkaline metals by seawater, made laboratory studies of gases from volcanic rocks, which he extracted from inclusions in crystals. Ten years later, the explorer Jean-Baptiste Boussingault (1802–87) tapped the fumaroles on Tolima and Puracé, two volcanoes in South America. In 1864 the German chemist Robert Bunsen (1811–99), accompanied by Sartorius von Waltershausen and the French mineralogist Alfred Des Cloizeaux (1817–97), explored the volcanoes of Iceland. There Sartorius discovered deposits of yellow tuff (rock made from volcanic material) that bore a strong resemblance to those he had observed to the south of Etna, which are caused by submarine eruptions: "the palagonites." Bunsen and Des Cloizeaux analyzed the hot springs, studied their chemical composition, and proposed a theory of how Geysir (or the Great Geyser) functioned. They climbed Hekla, just after its eruption in 1845, and tapped the gases that escaped from the still-smoking flows.

A descent into the crater of Hekla in 1868 (above). Below: Etna in 1852. Gases are the motive force of every eruption. They bring up the magma and are exhaled at the surface.

Charles Sainte-Claire Deville (1814–76) Was the True Originator of Gas Analyses of Volcanoes

In 1842, during his tour of the Canary Islands, the Antilles, and the Cape Verde Islands, the French mineralogist Charles Sainte-Claire Deville became interested in the sulfuric fumes being emitted from the dome of Soufrière (4813 feet) on Guadeloupe, in the West Indies, and he observed the formation of sulfur crystals. He continued his research in Italy. Witnessing the eruption of Vesuvius in 1855, he risked his life to take samples of the gaseous emanations at every phase of activity, from the paroxysm right through to its decline.

Until this point, it had been generally believed that every volcano was characterized by a different type of gas: sulfur dioxide on Etna, hydrochloric acid on Vesuvius, and carbon dioxide in the craters of the Andes. Sainte-Claire Deville now showed that, on the contrary, the same gases exist in every active volcano, but that their proportions change during the different phases of activity. He also demonstrated a relationship between the chemical composition of the gases and their temperature.

Fouqué, his pupil, studied the gases of Santorin, Etna's eruption in 1865, the fumaroles of Tuscany,

Above: A colored engraving of geysers in Iceland.

Geysers (from an Icelandic word meaning "to spring up") have given their name to all of the world's gushing springs. They are caused by explosive boiling water that accumulates in a vertical duct and is progressively heated from below. At the bottom of the shaft the water becomes several degrees hotter than boiling point, but it cannot boil because of the pressure of the column of water above and therefore is in an unstable superheated state. It requires only a minute disturbance, like an extra application of heat or a few gas bubbles, to make it vaporize instantly and explosively: It can expand abruptly to 1500 times its former volume.

and the thermal springs of the Azores. He was the first to recognize that hydrogen originates in the earth's depths. He also discovered that the flames exhaled by the flows of Santorin are a mixture of hydrogen and methane and demonstrated the importance of steam to the volcanic process.

Ernest Shepherd preparing to collect gases from the lava lake of Kilauea in Hawaii in 1912 (above). There, water vapor predominates, followed by carbon dioxide, sulfur dioxide, and hydrogen.

Is There Water in Volcanoes? If So, Where Does It Come From?

At the beginning of the 20th century, French chemist Emile Gautier (1837–1920) tried to prove, through experiments on granite and volcanic glass, that the water in volcanoes escapes from melting crystals. Many volcanologists today believe that it is surface water—rainwater or seawater—that infiltrates the earth's crust to great depths and then reemerges through volcanoes. The issue is still being debated.

Conversely, in 1911 the Swiss pharmacist Albert Brun (1857–1939) affirmed that there was no water in volcanic gases. It was just the humidity of the air which condensed as it came into contact with hot volcanic plumes. But two American geophysicists, Arthur Day (1869–1960) and Ernest Shepherd (1879–1949), proved that the amount of condensation that occurs is not sufficient to account for all the water present. In 1912 Day and Shepherd succeeded in taking samples of practically uncontaminated gases from the lake of molten lava at Kilauea, Hawaii. In their analysis, which is still a standard work today, they discovered that water vapor was the predominant component of the gases.

Volcanic Rocks Yielded Their Secrets

Until then, the study of rocks (petrography) had been done by naked eye and with magnifying glass. If the science had been more advanced at the time of the quarrel between Neptunists and Plutonists, they would quickly have realized that the truth lay with Hutton and his distinction between Plutonic rocks from the earth's depths and volcanic rocks from its surface.

The French mineralogist Pierre Cordier (1777–1862) introduced the first modern innovation when he pulverized rocks to separate their minerals, which he then classified by microscope according to their different

A thin section of a lava from Santorin, collected by Fouqué, is depicted in these lithographs as it is seen powerfully magnified under the microscope, in natural light (above) and polarized light (below). Lava, a pasty mass rich in gas bubbles and suspended crystals, has a complex chemical composition. It has absolutely nothing to do with carbon, bitumen, or sulfur, as was believed for a long time. Basalt, the best-known volcanic rock, is composed in atomic weight of about 45 percent oxygen, 23 percent silicon, 9 percent iron, 8 percent aluminum, 6 percent calcium, 4 percent magnesium, 2 percent sodium, 1 percent potassium, 1 percent titanium, and 1 percent various other components. The atoms are assembled in the rock in complex groupings called silicate minerals. Volcanologists generally classify volcanic rocks according to their silica content.

densities. But an even greater discovery was made by the Scottish physicist William Nicol (1768–1851). In 1828, while cutting thin transparent slices of fossilized wood, Nicol noticed the light-polarizing properties of the glasslike sections, and soon thereafter invented the polarizing microscope. For a time the scientific community ignored this significant contribution to science. But in 1850 English geologist Henry Sorby (1826–1908) was inspired by Nicol's work and used a polarizing microscope to observe thin sections, three hundredths of a millimeter thick, cut from volcanic rocks. An amazing sight! At last one could penetrate to the heart of the crystalline structure. The discovery had a great impact, and modern petrography was born. Soon Ferdinand Zirkel (1838–1912) and Harry Rosenbusch (1836–1914), both German geologists, and then American geologist Henry Washington (1867–1934),

Above: Kilauea's lake of lava in 1881.

Below: The andesite dome of Merapi, Java.

proposed new classifications of volcanic rocks based on chemical analysis and microscopic study.

At the end of the 19th century, Fouqué and another French scholar, Auguste Michel-Lévy (1844–1911), raised petrography to a full-fledged science and determined the optical characteristics of hundreds of minerals. There were plenty of detractors: "You can't study mountains with a microscope, and a thin section of less than a square centimeter cannot synthesize the history of a rock," stated one geologist.

Fouqué and Michel-Lévy pressed on with their research and produced the first minerals and rocks in a laboratory furnace. They artificially created feldspars, peridots, and pyroxenes, as well as andesites, basalts, and many other rocks, confirming the influence of cooling speed on the degree of crystallization. Later, experimental petrology (the study of molten silicates) was developed by Norman Bowen (1887–1956), an American petrologist, in the laboratory of the Carnegie Institution in Washington, D.C.

Volcanological Research Spread Throughout the World

In 1831 Charles Darwin (1809–82) set sail on the *Beagle*. With him he carried *The Principles of Geology* by Lyell, whom he greatly admired. This voyage, which lasted five years, took him to South America and the islands of the Pacific. Darwin was able to prove that the Pacific atolls surround the peaks of old volcanoes that have gradually sunk below the ocean.

Ten years later James Dana (1813–95), an American mineralogist and zoologist, joined an expedition led by his compatriot Charles Wilkes (1798–1877). Six ships set off intending to sail for three years in the South Pacific. The voyage actually lasted six years. Dana, who was in charge of geological studies, explored the Atlantic and the coasts of South America and landed in New Zealand and on many Pacific islands. In Hawaii he studied the volcanoes Kilauea and Mauna Loa, whose eruptions had already been described by resident missionaries such as Titus Coan (1801–82). Coan

The *Illustrated London News* depicted the lava fountain of the summit eruption of Mauna Loa in Hawaii, on 10 August 1872, as a fantasy: A mixture of a lava fountain, a geyser, and a firework.

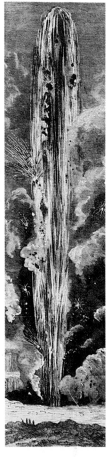

followed all the island's volcanic activities between 1835 and 1882 and described them in minute detail.

From the mid-19th century on, there were ever-increasing numbers of explorations of other volcanic regions of the globe.

Seismographs and Observatories

Modern volcanology began at the end of the 19th century. It made progress in fits and starts through the application of new techniques to the study of active volcanoes and the creation of volcanological observatories. In 1880 British scientists Thomas Gray and Sir Alfred Ewing invented the vertical-motion seismograph, a decisive event for the geophysics of volcanoes.

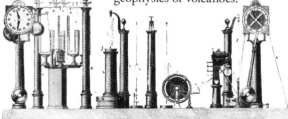

The first volcanological observatory was created at Vesuvius in 1841 by Ferdinand II, King of the Two Sicilies. The observatory's first director, Macedonio Melloni (1798–1854), was a specialist in the magnetism of volcanic rocks. His successors were great volcanologists: Luigi Palmieri (1807–96), inventor of an early seismograph that was used during the eruption

In November 1883, the Krakatau eruption caused sunsets in some parts of the world to be flaming red. Above: Views from London. The particles of pulverized lava rose into the stratosphere and encircled the globe, causing unusual diffractions of light.

By studying changes in topography, analyzing material ejected in the eruption, and listening to sailors who had been cruising in the island's waters at the end of August 1883, scientists were able to reconstruct the different phases of the catastrophe of Krakatau.

Above left: A seismograph invented by Palmieri to study Vesuvius.

of 1872; Raffaele Matteucci, initiator of measurements of distortion on the flanks of the volcano, who observed the cataclysm of Vesuvius in 1906; Giuseppe Mercalli (1850–1914), father of the scale of intensity of seismic shocks that bears his name. For several years two other observatories also monitored Vesuvius: One was set up by Immanuel Friedländer (1871–1948), a German patron of volcanology; the other was financed by the Pope and entrusted to Giovanni Battista Alfano (1878–1955), a priest known primarily for his studies on St. Januarius' blood.

One of the few depictions of the eruption (below) is based on a photograph taken on 27 July 1883, a month before the main paroxysm.

26–28 August 1883: Krakatau Exploded

Thirty-six thousand people in western Java died, drowned in the tidal waves—some as high as 50 feet—caused by the explosions of the Indonesian volcano. Sounds from the explosion were heard as far away as Istanbul, Australia, the Philippines, and Japan. Sunrises and sunsets were affected for several months following the eruption. The Dutch government sent a geologist to investigate the causes of the cataclysm, and the Royal Society of London set up a committee to study the geomorphological changes of the Krakatau archipelago after

the paroxysm, as well as the more distant effects, such as tidal waves, barometric shock waves, and ash in the upper atmosphere. This was the first time that such a large-scale study was ever undertaken.

In 1902 La Soufrière, Mount Pelée, and Santa Maria Were in the News

A black year: 1500, 28,000, and 6000 victims, respectively. These catastrophes, widely covered by the press, stirred the interest of several young volcanologists who established their reputations in the first half of the 20th century. The German geographer Karl Sapper (1866–1945) excelled in the study of Santa Maria in Guatemala. The eruption of La Soufrière was

The eruption of Mount Pelée, on Martinique, on 8 May 1902 was by far the most catastrophic of the century. Even today it continues to prevent the development of the new town of Saint-Pierre, which is no more than a shadow of the "Paris of the Antilles" that it was before the cataclysm. A small museum there displays a collection of photographs of the event, including the ash flows of 16 December 1902 (left) photographed by Alfred Lacroix and a number of objects melted in the fire caused by the ash flow of 8 May (above).

described in detail by the Englishmen Tempest
Anderson (1846–1913), a surgeon and volcanologist, and John Flett (1869–1947), a geologist.
They also went to Mount Pelée after its eruption
on 8 May, and observed, on 9 July, avalanches of
ash and rock and gases at temperatures of 200° to
900° C coming down the slopes at enormous speed—
and stopping only a few hundred yards from their boat.

These Ash Flows and the Growth of a Spine of Viscous Lava Were Studied by Mineralogist Francois-Antoine Alfred Lacroix

A professor at the natural history museum in Paris,
Lacroix (1863–1948) was sent to Martinique by the
French government. He described the results of his
research in a monumental work, *Mount Pelée and Its
Eruptions,* which was to bring him fame and contribute
greatly to his election to the French Academy of
Sciences in 1904. He said, with some humor: "I
entered the Institute through the irresistible thrust of a
volcano." He proposed the classification of the different
kinds of eruption still in use today: Hawaiian,

Lacroix (above)
was the author
of seven hundred
publications, including
a vast *Mineralogy of
France* and monographs
on Vesuvius and La
Fournaise that are still
authoritative today. He
married the daughter
of his mentor, Fouqué,
who agreed to the
marriage only after
Lacroix' thesis was
accepted. She
accompanied him on
almost all his travels
(above, in the ash and
rock deposits of Mount
Pelée), serving as his
secretary and sometimes
providing human scale
in his photographs.

Strombolian, Peléean, Vulcanian. Lacroix' photographs of Mount Pelée and its ash flows are still well known.

"These Thousands of People Killed by an Unknown Subterranean Phenomenon That Is Unexplained by the Geologists Deserve a Lifetime's Study"

American petrographer Thomas Augustus Jaggar (1871–1953) was among the first scientists to reach the scene after the eruption of Mount Pelée in 1902, and it was in the still-smoking ruins of Saint-Pierre that his vocation for volcanology was born. In 1906 he was actually at Vesuvius when it erupted, and he became increasingly convinced that permanent volcanological observatories are necessary for understanding volcanism and avoiding human deaths. Three years later he visited Tarumai and Asama in Japan when they erupted, before going to Kilauea in Hawaii in the company of his colleague Reginald Daly (1871–1957).

Thomas Jaggar Founded the Hawaiian Volcano Observatory Beside Kilauea

This observatory is today one of the greatest laboratories for the monitoring and prediction of eruptions. It took Jaggar three years to bring his project to fruition. In the

The catastrophe of Mount Pelée, with the destruction of the town of Saint-Pierre and its thousands of inhabitants, was front-page news. Below: A 1902 illustration.

meantime, in 1911, his collaborators, including Ernest
Shepherd, carried out the first measurement of the
temperature of a lake of molten lava, that of Kilauea. In
1912 the observatory was at last constructed, and
Jaggar settled in Hawaii for good, to the regret of his
colleagues at the Massachusetts Institute of Technology,
where he had been director of the geology department.
He recorded his observations of Kilauea and Mauna
Loa in *Volcano Letters.*

For the first few years, an association of amateurs,
supported by a local newspaper, the *Honolulu
Advertiser,* supplied part of the observatory's financing.
But after five years money was running short, so Jaggar
made up the difference by raising pigs. In 1919, to his
great relief, the observatory became a United States
national laboratory, thereafter to be
funded by the government.

Jaggar (opposite above)
was one of the first
volcanologists to
understand that contact
between lava and
groundwater could be
very explosive: This
phenomenon, called
hydromagmatism, is
well illustrated by the
explosive phase of Kilauea
in 1924 (above). A genius
at gadgetry, Jaggar
invented many scientific
instruments and, for
an expedition in
Alaska, designed an
amphibious vehicle,
the Honokai (below).

Frank Perret (1867–1943), Volcanological Engineer

A former engineer, inventor
of electrical motors, and
assistant to Thomas Alva
Edison (1847–1931), Perret
had set up a small business
enterprise to market his

inventions. But being of delicate health, he was obliged to take a rest from his activities. He traveled to Naples and there became friends with Raffaele Matteucci, director of the volcanological observatory of Vesuvius. He also witnessed the eruption of 1906. It was love at first sight.

Perret's ingenuity is legendary. Lacking a seismograph, he monitored the frequency of the small shocks that continually shake the flanks of Vesuvius by clamping his teeth over the metal frame of his bed, which was set in cement. This

La DOMENICA DEL CORRIERE

transmitted the slightest tremor to the teeth, which are particularly sensitive to vibrations.

By Observing Eruptive Phenomena, Perret Established Himself as a Great Volcanologist

Thus in 1907 he was able to correctly announce to the authorities that the worst of an eruption of Stromboli, in the Lipari Islands, had passed and that it was not necessary to evacuate the island's 4000 inhabitants. The following year he predicted an eruption of Etna. He was in Japan in 1914 and witnessed the paroxysm of Sakurajima.

During a later eruption of Mount Pelée in 1929–30 Perret observed and photographed the ash flows from a little hut less than 100 feet from the phenomenon. One of the flows even enveloped him in its cloud, but he survived. By getting to know the volcano so closely, at the risk of his own life, his knowledge of Mount Pelée's

Perret (opposite) testing his device for listening to underground noises. His model of Stromboli (below), using ammonia and hydrochloric acid, could produce plumes and coils of smoke.

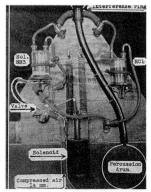

activities was so great that he felt able to reassure the local authorities that the town of Saint-Pierre was not under threat and that it was unnecessary to evacuate it. This accurate evaluation made him a local hero. A statue of him was even erected. Perret correctly claimed that gases are the motor force behind every volcanic eruption and that magma is merely the vehicle.

In 1932, at the insistence of Alfred Lacroix, the French authorities decided to turn the meteorological observation post of Morne des Cadets, set up near Mount Pelée in 1902, into a volcanological observatory.

Many other important volcanic events took place after the 1902 cataclysm of Mount Pelée. In 1912, the eruption in the Valley of Ten Thousand Smokes occurred without witnesses in the remote reaches of southwestern Alaska. Nearly 4 cubic miles of pumice flows filled an enormous valley, and the volcano Mount

A black year for the Naples region: 1906. Two illustrations testify to this: The Vesuvius observatory buried under impressive ash deposits, with Professor Matteucci on the steps (above); and the cover of an Italian weekly showing the inhabitants of Torre del Greco fleeing the terrible ash falls (opposite above).

Frank Perret was not only an outstanding volcanologist and an inventor of genius, but also a great photographer of erupting volcanoes. His work on the 1906 eruption of Vesuvius and the ash flows of Mount Pelée in 1929–30, as well as his volcanological observations worldwide, are illustrated with his own photographs, often taken at enormous risk.

Katmai had collapsed, creating a great caldera. The site was difficult to access and was only reached four years later by an expedition of the National Geographic Society. The products of the eruption would later be studied by researchers from the geophysical laboratory of the Carnegie Institution, one of whom recognized that the deposit contained an enormous sandy flow that had spread out at high temperature and great speed, an ash flow somewhat reminiscent of that of Mount Pelée in 1902, but gigantic. Two others analyzed the gas and sublimates that escaped from the deposit.

In 1914 it was the turn of On-take, in Japan, to awake abruptly. Here geologist Bundjiro Koto (1856–1935) and seismologist Fusakichi Omori (1868–1923) distinguished themselves brilliantly.

Volcanoes Under Intense Surveillance

In 1928 the first Japanese volcanological observatory was built at Aso, a volcano on Kyushu Island. It was followed by that of Asama, northwest of Tokyo— where Takeshi Minakami (1909–85), author of a classification of earthquakes of volcanic origin that is still in use today, did distinguished work; then observations were built at Sakurajima and Usu. All these observatories are now among the world's

The Japanese geophysicist Fusakichi Omori (below) described the growth of a dome on Usu in 1910 and the explosive activities of Asama. His work with seismographs made them popular for use with volcanoes. He studied the ground distortions caused by eruptions by means of inclinometers. He is said to have died of grief after the earthquake of 1 September 1923 ravaged Tokyo.

most modern, dealing electronically with thousands of pieces of information every moment.

Before the Second World War, the Dutch also created numerous observation posts on the volcanoes of Indonesia, soon to be followed by the Russians at Kamchatka, the Australians at Rabaul in New Guinea, and many others.

Although one of the first volcanoes to be studied, Etna was one of the last to be given scientific attention in the modern age. It was not until 1953 that, on the initiative of a Swiss volcanologist, Alfred Rittmann (1893–1981), the International Institute of Volcanological Research was created to monitor Etna.

In 1943 two new volcanoes arose, the cone of Parícutin in a cornfield in Mexico, and the dome of Showa-Shinzan in Japan, but the events went almost unnoticed in the world because of the war. The birth of the volcanic island of Surtsey in the Atlantic south of Iceland in 1963 was to enable that country's volcanologists to witness firsthand every phase of an eruption at sea.

The contribution of Icelandic volcanologists was essential, especially that of Sigurdur Thorarinsson (1911–83), who developed tephrochronology, which uses the layers of ash ejected by a volcano as stratigraphic markers for dating eruptions.

The cataclysm of Bandai, on 15 July 1888, was studied in detail by Seikei Sekiya (1855–96) and Dairoku Kikuchi (1855–1917). The eruption began after a 15-minute seismic event. Major explosions, directed horizontally northward and accompanied by a column of ash over 2 miles high, shattered the volcano's cone in less than a minute. Immediately, its northern flank collapsed in one enormous avalanche accompanied by a horizontal blast that buried several villages, killed 461 peasants, and blocked several rivers, thus creating five new lakes. Above and opposite above: Prints showing the eruption and the devastation it caused.

The Three Major Events of the 1980s

On 18 May 1980 Mount Saint Helens, in Washington
State, collapsed and then exploded violently, throwing
a cloud of ash to a height of over 15 miles and releasing
a lateral blast with a speed of 620 miles per hour and a
temperature of over 300° C that destroyed everything
up to 18 miles north of the cone. The damage was
tremendous, but the number of victims was limited
because, on the advice of volcanologists, the danger
zone had been closed by the authorities. No explosive
eruption—involving ash and pulverized lava—had ever
been so well studied by the experts. The observatory in
the Cascades that monitored the event became for
explosive volcanism what the one on Hawaii has long
been for effusive—involving flows of lava—volcanism.

The 1982 cataclysm of El Chichón in Mexico sent
columns of ash and sulfurous gas to a height of 20
miles and marked a turning point in the study of the
climatic disturbances that are provoked by eruptions.

Finally, on 13 November 1985, explosions from
Nevado del Ruiz, in Colombia, brought about the
melting of its summit glacier, leading to enormous mud
flows that engulfed the nearby town of Armero and its
22,000 inhabitants, the most lethal catastrophe since
that of Mount Pelée in 1902. The eruption had been
predicted by volcanologists, but they were unable

to convince the authorities that the danger was imminent. The lesson is clear: Volcanology is not merely a science. It also involves humanitarian duties; volcanologists must inform an area's inhabitants of the risks and know how to convince the authorities that they must evacuate the threatened populations before it is too late.

Despite Its Enormous Progress, the Science of Volcanology Is Still in Its Infancy

We know today that magma's heat comes in large part from the natural radioactivity of rocks and that the distribution of volcanoes depends on plate tectonics. We also know how to date volcanic rocks by means of their radioactivity and hence how to trace their history. Studying the geochemistry of trace elements and isotopes (groups of similar atoms in a chemical element) is enabling us little by little to penetrate the secrets of the magma reservoirs. Predicting eruptions so as to be able to evacuate populations in time has become a reality, but only 150 active volcanoes are monitored by volcanological observatories, whereas we should be monitoring a thousand. It is becoming possible to limit the devastating effects of lava flows and mud flows. Surveillance of volcanoes by satellite seems to be a promising development. But we still have no general theory of volcanism that might allow us at last to know precisely why a volcano erupts. A formidable task awaits future generations of volcanologists.

EDITOR'S NOTE: For a description of the devastating eruption of Mount Pinatubo in the Philippines in June 1991, which occurred after the tragic death of the author, see page 192.

On 22 July 1980, at 6:25 PM, a heavy plume of ash, rocks, and gas rose majestically above Mount Saint Helens (opposite left). Two months earlier a blast with a speed of nearly 685 miles per hour and a temperature of 300° C had, in a few moments, buried this car (above) in ash and killed its driver, even though it was over 7 miles from the crater.

The eruption of Eldfell volcano on Heimaey Island (left and overleaf), south of Iceland, began on 23 January 1973 at 1:55 AM. A fissure 5900 feet long opened near the town, and lava fountained out (opposite right). The volcano had not erupted for 5000 years.

DOCUMENTS

"...as when the force
Of subterranean wind transports a hill
Torn from Pelorus, or the shattered side
Of thundering Aetna, whose combustible
And fuelled entrails thence conceiving fire,
Sublimed with mineral fury, aid the winds,
And leave a singed bottom all involved
With stench and smoke...."

John Milton, *Paradise Lost,* 1667

The Poem *Aetna*

After mocking those who believe in the story of the forges of Vulcan, an unknown ancient Roman poet tries to explain the geophysical basis for the eruptions of Etna.

Winds: The Cause of the Mountain's Eruptions

On this side are vast openings which terrify and plunge in an abyss, on another side the mountain rearranges its limbs projected too far. Elsewhere thick crags bar the path, and enormous is the confusion....

A cloud of burnt sand is driven in a whirl; swiftly rush the flaming masses; from the depth foundations are upheaved. Now bursts a crash from Aetna everywhere: now the flames show ghastly pale as they mingle with the dark downpour....

It is the winds which arouse all these forces of havoc: The rocks which they have massed thickly

A 17th-century depiction of Etna erupting.

together they whirl in eddying storm and roll from the abyss…fire has always a natural velocity and perpetual motion, but some ally is needed for the propulsion of bodies. In itself it has no motive energy: Where spirit is commander, it obeys. Spirit is emperor: Fire serves in the army of this great captain.…

Sulfur, Alum, Bitumen, and Especially Lava-stone Feed the Eruptions

Now there remain to be discussed all the materials which govern the conflagration, what fuels summon the flames, what is Aetna's food.… At one time the hot liquid of sulphur burns continuously; at another a fluid presents itself thickened with copious alum; oily bitumen is at hand and everything that by close encounter provokes flames to violence.…

The Character of Lava-stone: Strong But Submissive

But the paramount source of that volcanic fire is the lava-stone. It above all claims Aetna for its own. If perchance you held it in your hand and tested it by its firmness, you would not think it could burn or discharge fire, but no sooner do you question it with iron than it replies, and sparks attest its pain beneath the blow.

Throw it in the midst of a strong fire, and let it wrest away its proud temper: So strip it of its strength. It will fuse quicker than iron, for its nature is subject to change and afraid of hurt under pressure from fire.…

Every other substance productive of fire dies after it has been lighted: Nothing remains therein to be recovered—merely ashes and earth with not a seed of flame. But this lava-stone, submissive time and again, after absorbing a thousand fires, renews its strength.…

The Various Phases of an Eruption

Then shall you think fit to flee in panic and yield place to the divine event.

From the safety of a hill you will be able to observe all. For on a sudden the conflagration blazes out, loaded with its spoils; masses of burning matter advance; mutilated lumps of falling rock roll forth and whirl dark shoals of sand. They present vague shapes in human likeness—some of the stones suggest the defeated warrior, some a gallant host armed for a standing fight, unassailed by the flames.…

But when a heap has gradually sprung up raised from fallen rocks, they mount in a narrow-pointed pyramid. Just as a stone is calcined in a furnace and its moisture all burnt out inside and through the pores it steams on high, so the lava-stone loses its substance and is turned out a light pumice of inconsiderable weight: The lava-liquid begins to boil hotter and at last to advance more in the fashion of a gentle stream, as it lets its waves course down the slopes of the hills. By stages the waves advance some twice six miles.

Nay, nothing can recall them: Nothing checks these determined fires: No mass can hold them—'tis vain: All is war together.

Translated by J. Wight Duff and Arnold M. Duff, 1954

The Eruption of Vesuvius in AD 79

In AD 104 Roman author Pliny the Younger (61–c. 113) wrote two letters to Tacitus in which he tells of the circumstances under which his uncle, Pliny the Elder (b. AD 23), was killed during the brutal awakening of Vesuvius in the year 79. Pliny the Younger, then eighteen years old, witnessed the eruption and describes its phases with great accuracy.

Extract from the First Letter

He [Pliny the Elder] was at that time with the fleet under his command at Misenum [a port in the Bay of Naples]. On the 24th of August, about one in the afternoon, my mother desired him to observe a cloud of very unusual size and appearance.... It was not at that distance discernible from what mountain this cloud issued, but it was found afterwards to be Vesuvius [in fact, Monte Somma]. I cannot give you a more exact description of its figure than by resembling it to that of a pine-tree, for it shot up a great height in the form of a trunk, which extended itself at the top into several branches [a Plinian plume]; because, I imagine, a momentary gust of air blew it aloft, and then failing, forsook it; thus causing the cloud to expand laterally as it dissolved, or possibly the downward pressure of its own weight produced this effect. It was at one moment white, at another dark and spotted, as if it had carried up earth or cinders.

My uncle, true savant that he was, deemed the phenomenon important and worth a nearer view. He ordered a light vessel to be got ready, and gave me the liberty...to attend him. I replied I would rather study....

Hastening to the place from whence others were flying, he steered his direct course to the point of danger, and with such freedom from fear, as to be able to make and dictate his observations upon the successive motions and figures of that terrific object. And now cinders, which grew thicker and hotter the nearer he approached, fell into the ships, then pumice-stones too, with

Pliny the Younger.

stones blackened, scorched, and cracked by fire, then the sea ebbed suddenly from under them, while the shore was blocked up by landslips from the mountains. After considering a moment whether he should retreat, he said to the captain who was urging that course, "Fortune befriends the brave; carry me to Pomponianus." Pomponianus was then at Stabiae, distant by half the width of the bay....

In the meanwhile Mount Vesuvius was blazing in several places with spreading and towering flames whose refulgent brightness the darkness of the night set in high relief. But my uncle, in order to soothe apprehensions, kept saying that some fires had been left alight by the terrified country people, and what they saw were only deserted villas on fire in the abandoned district. After this he retired to rest, and it is most certain that his rest was a most genuine slumber; for his breathing, which, as he was pretty fat, was somewhat heavy and sonorous, was heard by those who attended at his chamber-door. But the court which led to his apartment now lay so deep under a mixture of pumice-stones and ashes, that if he had continued longer in his bedroom, egress would have been impossible. On being aroused, he came out, and returned to Pomponianus and the others, who had sat up all night. They consulted together as to whether they should hold out in the house, or wander about in the open. For the house now tottered under repeated and violent concussions, and seemed to rock to and fro as if torn from its foundations. In the open air, on the other hand, they dreaded the falling pumice-stones, light and porous though they were; yet this, by comparison,

seemed the lesser danger of the two; a conclusion which my uncle arrived at by balancing reasons, and the others by balancing fears. They tied pillows upon their heads with napkins; and this was their whole defence against the showers that fell round them.

It was now day everywhere else, but there a deeper darkness prevailed than in the most obscure night; relieved, however, by many torches and diverse illuminations. They thought proper to go down upon the shore to observe from close at hand if they could possibly put out to sea, but they found the waves still ran extremely high and contrary. There my uncle having thrown himself down upon a disused sail, repeatedly called for, and drank, a draught of cold water; soon after, flames, and a strong smell of sulphur, which was the forerunner of them, dispersed the rest of the company in flight; him they only aroused. He raised himself up with the assistance of two of his slaves, but instantly fell; some unusually gross vapour, as I conjecture, having obstructed his breathing and blocked his windpipe, which was not only naturally weak and constricted, but chronically inflamed. When day dawned again (the third from that he last beheld) his body was found entire and uninjured, and still fully clothed as in life; its posture was that of a sleeping, rather than a dead man....

Extract from the Second Letter

My uncle having set out, I gave the rest of the day to study....

There had been for several days before some shocks of earthquake, which the less alarmed us as they are frequent in Campania; but that night they became so violent that one might

The death of Pliny the Elder.

think that the world was not being merely shaken, but turned topsy-turvy. My mother flew to my chamber; I was just rising, meaning on my part to awaken her, if she was asleep. We sat down in the forecourt of the house, which separated it by a short space from the sea.…

It was now six o'clock in the morning, the light still ambiguous and faint. The buildings around us already tottered, and though we stood upon open ground, yet as the place was narrow and confined, there was certain and formidable danger from their collapsing. It was not till then we resolved to quit the town. The common people follow us in the utmost consternation…and impel us onwards by pressing in a crowd upon our rear. Being got outside the houses, we halt in the midst of a most strange and dreadful scene. The coaches which we had ordered out, though upon the most level ground, were sliding to and fro, and could not be kept steady even when stones were put against the wheels. Then we beheld the sea sucked back, and as it were repulsed by the convulsive motion of the earth [a retreat of the water that precedes a tidal wave]; it is certain at least the shore was considerably enlarged, and now held many sea animals captive on the dry sand. On the other side, a black and dreadful cloud bursting out in gusts of igneous serpentine vapour now and again yawned open to reveal long fantastic flames, resembling flashes of lightning but much larger [the static electricity of the ash columns].... Soon afterwards the cloud I have described began to descend upon the earth, and cover the sea.... My mother now began to beseech, exhort, and command me to escape as best I might; a young man could do it; she, burdened with age and corpulency, would die easy if only she had not caused my death. I replied, I would not be saved without her....

Ashes now fall upon us, though as yet in no great quantity. I looked behind me; gross darkness pressed upon our rear, and came rolling over the land after us like a torrent [an ash flow]. I proposed while we yet could see, to turn aside, lest we should be knocked down in the road by the crowd that followed us and trampled to death in the dark. We had scarce sat down, when darkness overspread us, not like that of a moonless or cloudy night, but of a room when it is shut up, and the lamp put out. You could hear the shrieks of women, the crying of children, and the shouts of men....

By degrees it grew lighter; which we imagined to be rather the warning of approaching fire (as in truth it was) than the return of day: However, the fire stayed at a distance from us: then again came darkness, and a heavy shower of ashes; we were obliged every now and then to rise and shake them off, otherwise we should have been buried and even crushed under their weight. I might have boasted that amidst dangers so appalling, not a sigh or expression of fear escaped from me, had not my support been founded in that miserable, though strong consolation, that all mankind were involved in the same calamity....

At last this dreadful darkness was attenuated by degrees to a kind of cloud or smoke, and passed away; presently the real day returned, and even the sun appeared, though lurid as when an eclipse is in progress. Every object that presented itself to our yet affrighted gaze was changed, covered over with a drift of ashes, as with snow. We returned to Misenum, where we refreshed ourselves as well as we could, and passed an anxious night between hope and fear; though indeed with a much larger share of the latter, for the earthquake still continued, and several enthusiastic people were giving a grotesque turn to their own and their neighbours' calamities by terrible predictions. Even then, however, my mother and I...had no thoughts of leaving the place, till we should receive some tidings of my uncle....

The Letters of Pliny
translated by William Melmoth
revised by W. M. L. Hutchinson
1915 (reprinted in 1927)

Volcanoes in France

In 1751 Jean-Etienne Guettard (1715–86) made one of the greatest discoveries in French volcanology—that there were volcanoes in the Massif Central, a plateau region in central France. His findings prompted him to muse, "It thus seems, from these various observations, that [the regions of] Auvergne and Dauphiné contain a great number of mountains that have burned. But at what period did they undergo these terrible effects?"

HISTOIRE
DE
L'ACADEMIE ROYALE
DES SCIENCES.
Année M. DCCLII.

PHYSIQUE GENERALE.

*SUR QUELQUES MONTAGNES DE FRANCE
QUI ONT ETE VOLCANS.*

At a time when the earth seems to be in a state of fermentation, one may perhaps not be sorry to learn that this kingdom, in far-off centuries, had volcanoes at least as terrible as those I have just mentioned, and which perhaps require only the slightest cause and movement to burst into flames again. Is this knowledge not preferable to the security in which we are living?

And if it reminds us of our ancestors' misfortunes, might it not also be to our advantage by stimulating us to seek to determine those mountains of France which have burned in the past? Quite apart from the views on general physics that might be deduced from this, might not this knowledge and the comparison that can be made between these places and those which were never affected instill a justifiable fear in the inhabitants of the cantons where there are extinct volcanoes… and encourage them, on the occasion of earthquakes, to take the precautions that it is never shameful and always wise to take at such times?…

The mountains that, I believe, used to be volcanoes as terrible as those of today, are those of Volvic, two leagues from Riom; the Puy de Dôme, near Clermont; and Mont-Dore. The volcano of Volvic was formed by its lava—which must have been made of molten materials like that of Vesuvius; different lava beds piled up on top of each other and hence comprised enormous masses into which stone quarries have been dug at several places quite far from Volvic. The building housing the fountains of Vichy, the basin of Caesar's baths at Mont-Dore, the houses of Clermont, the basins of that town's public fountains and those of Moulins in the Bourbonnais are all made of this stone.

It was at Moulins that I saw the lava for the first time: I first recognized it as made from volcanic stones, and I believed henceforth that there must have been a volcano in the region from which I was told these stones had been brought. My desire to see this area was only increased in the various places to which the road led me and where I kept finding this stone used for building.

Having at last arrived at Riom, I could scarcely believe that this town was almost entirely built of this stone, since the quarries were far away, but I then learned that they were at a distance of only two leagues. I would have considered it a great loss if I had not seen this place, so I went there. I had not even begun to climb the mountain that dominates Volvic when I recognized that it was almost completely composed of the different materials that are ejected during volcanic eruptions.

This mountain looks just like the volcanoes in the descriptions of them that we have: It is conical, its base is formed of rocks of gray-white or pale pink granite which are very hard and take on quite a fine polish; the rest of the mountain is a mere mass of blackish or reddish pumice stones, piled up on each other with no order or bonding. These stones take on a rounded appearance. Some are only the size of gravel, others exceed the size of a man's head; on two-thirds of the mountain, one encounters irregular rocks, bristling with shapeless points, twisted in all directions. These rocks resemble scoria, especially as they are a dark red or a dirty, dull black; they are of a hard,

solid substance and differ in this from pumice stones, which are full of holes of various sizes and hence almost like sponges.

In the space between these rocks and the top of the mountain, one is again walking on pumice stones, and at the summit one finds a soft, ashy stone. It is not in little separate masses, like pumice stones, but it forms such big masses as to be considered a kind of rock. Shortly before reaching the summit, one enters a broad hole that is conical in shape and almost like a funnel…. This hole, like the scoria, faces southwest.

The part of the mountain that is on the north and east seemed to me to be composed only of pumice stone; to the west the ravines displayed considerable layers of stones, tilted to the horizon, that seem to extend over the mountain's full height….

This stone is hard, albeit spongy; its holes are small, irregular, of different shapes and diameters; the quantity of these holes makes the stone more or less solid, and makes it seem to be of excellent quality….

Shortly after Clermont one begins to climb and continues to do so gradually up to the part of this mountain that is called the Puy de Dôme. This part is a cone that, like that of Volvic, ends in a small point. To the north and west of this peak are several others resembling this one in shape but much less high, although still quite high when compared to the mountains of the Paris region. These various cones are placed on the body of the mountain as on a common base….

This mountain is pleasant and beautiful to the eye; but when one takes a close look it displays only depressing and even terrifying objects. It is just a mass of matter that evokes the terrible effects of the most violent fire that is capable of reducing the hardest bodies to a state of such fusion that they form only a crude glass or a kind of slag of various shapes and weights. It was not difficult for me to recognize first of all that the Puy de Dôme, like Volvic, had once been a volcano. Everything points to this. In the areas that are not covered by plants and trees one walks solely on pumice stones, on fragments of lava, and on a kind of gravel or sand formed of a kind of slag and very small pumice stones mixed with ash....

I had found a funnel at the top of the Puy de Dôme and, as this peak dominates its neighbors, I had observed that near the summit of each peak there was a cavity whose bottom was less wide than its opening and which I believed to be the funnel or mouth of the volcano. Before climbing down the mountain I went to examine one of these funnels.

The peak, the track leading to it, and the entire area between there and the Puy de Dôme are one great heap of pumice stones like those of the Puy. I therefore felt it useless to go and examine the others, and I was further supported in my opinion by the fact that Mr. Ozy, an apothecary at Clermont who is well versed in natural history and who had agreed to accompany me, assured me that he had explored almost the whole mountain more than once and that in every part of it I would find the same structure and the same materials, which, he ingenuously confessed, he had never recognized for what they were....

There is, however, every reason to think that these funnels are the marks of different eruptions and that what happened in those days is what one observes today in volcanoes that eject flames.

The body of the mountain opens up at one or two places, the eruption continues through those mouths, and it is rare for it to make others while this eruption lasts. The flaming materials have found a few exits, they no longer fight against the mountain, but follow the route they have made, unless the inflammable materials spread over the body of the mountain so as to form different branches that can catch fire at the same time or in succession. Besides, whether those funnels on the mountain of the Puy de Dôme were made on one or on several occasions, one cannot doubt that this mountain has been burned over its entire length....

These reflections naturally lead me to wish to know the characteristics of stones caused by volcanoes and to develop this investigation further than I have done so far. I even need to delve into this research to establish beyond doubt that the mountains I claim to be extinct volcanoes really are what I believe them to be. Up to now I have drawn my proof from the fact that they are composed of pumice stones and lava, but I have not proved that these stones are volcanic. I can only acquire more definite proof by comparing them with similar materials taken from a mountain currently ablaze and looking at the relationship between them, right down to the smallest irregularities.

This comparison was made easy thanks to material ejected from

Vesuvius that I received from Mr. de Montigny and the Abbé Nollet and material from the volcano of Bourbon [Réunion] Island sent by the late Mr. Lieutaud, surgeon for the Compagnie des Indes.

The piece of surface lava from Vesuvius that I have—that is, of that type of scum that one sees swimming on the blazing streams that exit from the mouth of the volcano and that, on cooling, form lava—that piece, I say, is irregular in shape, full of tuberosities, dark gray in color, and covered with black dots. One can see a great number of these stones on the whole body of the mountains of our extinct volcanoes. Like those of Vesuvius they have black dots; there are also some with white dots, which may be spathic, and others are dark yellow....

It is not gratuitous to claim that there is bitumen in these mountains; the surroundings of volcanoes almost always have some. Those of Vesuvius, Etna, and Heda contain bituminous fountains or quarries of coal, jet, or bitumen....

The lightness of some blackish pumice stones is some proof of this. They have the exterior and lightness of the scoria that remains after the distillation of bitumen....

So everything combines to prove that the mountains to which this study is devoted were once ablaze, that they may still have a tendency to burst into flame.

Jean-Etienne Guettard,
*Records of the Royal Academy
of Sciences,*
1752

Basalt columns at Saint-Flour, France.

Sir William Hamilton, Field Volcanologist

British ambassador to the court of Naples and member of the Royal Society of London, Hamilton was enamored of Vesuvius, his "great laboratory of nature," which he observed from close at hand. He and others described its activities between 1764 and 1794.

1767: Hamilton Escaped Death on the Volcano, and Saint Januarius Stopped the Eruption

[I]...proceeded far in the valley between the mountain of Somma and that of Vesuvius, which is called *Atrio di Cavallo*. I was making my observations upon the lava...when on a sudden, about noon, I heard a violent noise within the mountain, and at about a quarter of a mile off the place where I stood, the mountain split and with much noise, from this new mouth a fountain of liquid fire shot up many feet high, and then like a torrent, rolled on directly towards us. The earth shook at the same time that a volley of pumice stones fell thick upon us; in an instant clouds of black [smoke] and ashes caused almost a total darkness; the explosions from the top of the mountain were much louder than any thunder I ever heard, and the smell of

Eruption of ashes from Vesuvius, 19 June 1794.

the sulphur was very offensive. My guide alarmed took to his heels; and I must confess that I was not at my ease. I followed close, and we ran near three miles without stopping; as the earth continued to shake under our feet, I was apprehensive of the opening of a fresh mouth, which might have cut off our retreat. I also feared that the violent explosions would detach [some] of the ro[c]ks of the mountain of Somma, under which we were obliged to pass; besides, the pumice-stones, falling upon us like hail, were of such a size as to cause a disagreeable sensation upon the part where they fell. After having taken breath, as the earth still trembled greatly, I thought it most prudent to leave the mountain....

Tuesday the 20th [of October]... small ashes fell all this day at Naples. The lava on both sides of the mountain ran violently; but there was little or no noise till about nine o'clock at night, when the same uncommon rumbling began again, accompanied with explosions as before, which lasted about four hours: It seemed as if the mountain would split in pieces; and indeed, it opened this night almost from the top to the bottom....

Thursday 22nd, about ten of the clock in the morning, the same thundering noise began again, but with more violence than the preceding days.... The ashes, or rather small cinders, showered down so fast that the people in the streets were obliged to use umbrellas or flap their hats, these ashes being very offensive to the eyes. The tops of the houses and the balconies were covered above an inch thick with these cinders.... In the midst of these horrors, the Mob growing tumultuous and impatient, obliged the Cardinal to

bring out the Head of Saint Januarius, and go with it in procession to the Ponte Maddalena, at the extremity of Naples, towards Vesuvius; and it is well attested here, that the eruption ceased the moment the Saint came in sight of the mountain.

Sir William Hamilton
Campi Phlegraei
1776

1779: A Fountain of Lava More Than 9000 Feet High and a Burial Beneath Ashes

On Thursday the 5th of August last, about two o'clock in the afternoon, I perceiv'd from my Villa at Pausilipo in the Bay of Naples, from whence I have a full view of Vesuvius (which is just opposite, and at the distance of about six miles in a direct line from it) that the Volcano was in a most violent agitation....

On Saturday August the 7th...its fermentation increased greatly....

Sunday August the 8th.... At about nine o'clock there was a loud report, which shook the houses at Portici and its neighbourhood to such a degree as to alarm their inhabitants, and drive them out into the streets.... In an instant a fountain of liquid tra[n]sparent fire began to rise, and gradually increasing arrived at so amazing a height as to strike every one who beheld it with the most awfull astonishment: I shall scarcely be credited, when I assure you, Sir, that to the best of my judgement the height of this stupendous column of fire could not be less than three times that of Vesuvius itself, which, as you know, rises perpendicularly, near 3700 feet above the level of the sea.

Puffs of smoke as black as can

possibly be imagined succeeded one another hastily, and accompanied the red hot transparent and liquid lava interrupting its splendid brightness here and there by patches of the darkest hue; within these puffs of smoke at the very moment of their emission from the crater I could perceive a bright but pale electrical fire briskly playing about in zigzag lines....

About five o'clock in the evening the eruption ceased. Some rain having fallen this day, which having been greatly impregnated with the corrosive salts of the Volcano did much damage to the vines in its neighbourhood... such a scene of desolation and misery, affording to our view nothing but heaps of black cinders, and ashes, blasted trees, ruined houses, with a few of their scattered inhabitants just return'd with ghastly, dismay'd countenances....

We proceeded from Caccia-bella to Ottaiano, which is a mile nearer to Vesuvius, and is reckon'd to contain twelve thousand inhabitants; nothing could be more dismal, than the sight of this town, unroofed, half burried under black scoriae and ashes, all the windows towards the Mountain broken, and some of the houses themselves burnt, the streets [choked] up with these ashes, (in some, that were narrow, the stratum was not less than four feet thick).

> Sir William Hamilton
> *Supplement to the Campi Phlegraei*
> 1779

1794: The Destruction of Torre del Greco and Flows to the Sea

The annexed view represents the destruction of the city of Torre del Greco, in June 1794, by an eruption of Vesuvius. The drawing, from which the engraving is made, was taken on the spot eight days after the destruction of the City, and is a faithful representation of that dreadful event.... The following account of this eruption is extracted from an interesting work on the present state of Vesuvius, by Breislack [a celebrated Italian geologist].

"On the 12th of June, 1794, towards eleven in the evening, a violent shock of an earthquake was felt, which induced many of the inhabitants of Naples to leave their houses for the night. The tranquillity of the mountain did not appear disturbed either on the 13th, 14th, or 15th, nor did it exhibit any symptom of an approaching eruption; but towards nine o'clock in the evening of the 15th, many symptoms were manifested. The houses about the mountain experienced violent shocks, which gradually increased; and a very powerful one was felt at ten o'clock in Naples and its environs. At this instant, on the eastern base of the cone, at the spot called La Pedamentina, and from the midst of ancient torrents, a new

mouth disgorged a stream of liquid fire. This opening was 2375 feet in length, and 237 in breadth....

"The lava flowed in one body for some time, and at intervals flashes of light arose from the surface of it....

"Its first direction was towards Portici and Resina, so that the inhabitants of Torre del Greco already bewailed the fate of their neighbours, and began their thanksgivings to the Almighty for their escape. Collected together in the Church, they were still singing hymns of joy, and expressing their gratitude, when a voice announced to them the fatal news of their approaching destiny. The stream of lava, on flowing down a declivity met in its way, divided itself into three branches.... The residue of the lava...flowed upon Torre, presenting a front from 1200 to 1500 feet in breadth, and filling several deep ravines. On reaching the first houses of the town, the stream divided according to the different slopes of the streets, and the degrees of opposition presented by the buildings....

"The vast clouds of thick black smoke which rose from the town, the flames occasionally crowning the summit of the houses, the ruins of the buildings, the noise of the falling palaces and houses, the rumbling of the volcano—these were the principal incidents of the horrible yet sublime scene. To these objects...was added another which forcibly touches the heart; this was a doleful group of 15,000 persons bewailing the destruction of their city...who had but a moment's notice to flee and abandon their homes for ever."

W. R., *The Gentleman's Magazine*, May 1822

This depiction of the destruction of Torre del Greco in June 1794 accompanied the 1822 article in *The Gentleman's Magazine*.

Priests Describe Hell

Until the mid-19th century, members of the clergy were great observers of eruptions. We owe to them not only the descriptions of most of the activities of Vesuvius and Etna but also those of the majority of great volcanic cataclysms throughout the world. Without them, we would have no written record of many eruptions.

M ap of the island of Lanzarote after the eruption of 1730–6.

Between 1730 and 1736, a formidable deluge poured over the island of Lanzarote in the Canary Islands. The priest of the town of Yaiza, Don Andrés Lorenzo Curbelo, helps us relive the cataclysm.

On 1 September 1730, between nine and ten in the evening, the earth suddenly opened near Timanfaya two leagues from Yaiza. On that first night an enormous mountain arose from the bosom of the earth, and from its summit there escaped flames that continued to burn for nineteen days…a torrent of lava rushed down to Timanfaya, Rodeo, and a part of Mancha Blanca. At first the lava spread over villages to the north as rapidly as water, but soon its speed slowed so that it flowed more like honey.…

On 11 September, the eruption was renewed with great force, and the lava began to flow again. From Santa Catalina it rushed down to Maso, burned and covered that whole village, and continued on its way to the sea; it flowed for six days in succession with a terrible din and formed real cataracts. A great quantity of dead fish floated on the surface of the sea.…

Soon all was calm again. But on 18 October, three new openings formed above Santa Catalina, which was still burning, and from its orifices there poured masses of a thick smoke that spread over the whole island.… The thunderclaps and explosions that accompanied these phenomena—and the darkness produced by the mass of ashes and smoke that covered the island—forced the inhabitants of Yaiza and neighboring places to flee more than once.…

By 28 October the volcanic activity had been going on in this way for ten whole days when suddenly the livestock fell dead, asphyxiated throughout the country by an emission of pestilential vapors that condensed and fell as droplets.

On 30 October peace returned.... But on 1 November the smoke and ashes began to appear again....

On the 27th another flow rushed with incredible speed toward the seashore; it reached it on 1 December and, in the midst of the waters, formed a small island which was completely surrounded by numerous dead fish....

On 16 December, the lava...reached Chupadero which soon, by the 17th, was one vast fire. It then ravaged the fertile Vega de Ugo....

On 7 January 1731 further eruptions devastated the earlier ones. Incandescent currents, accompanied by very thick smoke, came out of two openings...formed in the mountain. The clouds of smoke were frequently lit by brilliant flashes of a blue and red light, followed by violent thunderclaps, like in storms, and this spectacle was as terrifying as it was new for the inhabitants, because storms are unknown in these lands....

On 3 February a new cone rose up; it burned the village of Rodeo...!

On 7 March other cones arose and the lava that flowed from them... reached Tingafa, which was completely devastated....

Every time that the people thought their misfortunes were drawing to a close new fissures opened up, and new cones arose. There were even submarine eruptions....

This was too much; the inhabitants abandoned all hope and left for good with the priest of Yaiza to take refuge on the island of Gran Canaria. The earth continued to vomit its incandescent basalt until 16 April 1736, engulfing a surface of about 80 square miles, covering fields and villages, destroying 400 houses and building more than 30 cones that were all aligned on a gigantic fissure. The western quarter of the island, once so fertile and flourishing, was annihilated.

Father Giovanni-Maria Della Torre, author of History and Phenomena of Vesuvius, *told in minute detail of the volcano's eruptions and carried out some strange experiments. He took daring risks on his expeditions, such as this one during the eruption of 1767.*

The mountain was thundering in a terrible manner, and at each explosion quantities of stones became detached from the precipice of Somma and fell all around us. In that state we walked much more quickly than in a procession, but our guides, having prayed to St. Januarius and St. Anthony to take their place, left us very hurriedly and ran with all their might to the hermitage.

Soon we were regretting that we had not followed their example, because a cloud of sulfur enveloped us, and I really think that if it had lasted ten minutes we would all have perished. But luckily it passed very quickly. I believe this suffocating smoke was carried by the wind from the great mouth that had spewed out lava. Because at the same moment, through the smoke, we saw a shining ocean of liquid fire that seemed to have entirely filled the great valley separating the three mountains.

Struck by the magnificence of such an object, we stopped for a few moments, but the dilemma in which we found ourselves prevented us from enjoying it to the full. However, after holding a council of war, we decided that retreat would be very difficult, shameful, and dangerous, and that we absolutely must find some way to pass that red sea, so much more terrible than the one that engulfed Pharaoh and his army....

So we set ourselves to checking whether there was still a free passage at the foot of Somma, but to our great astonishment (not to say fear) it was already surrounded by lava. There was no alternative whatsoever. We were forced to climb the mountain slope and skirt the lava right to its extremity, which, we thought, was not very distant. The journey was very arduous, stones were falling around us, and the heat of the lava was often excessive and had already set ablaze all the brush on the mountain slope....

We descended via Otayane and arrived at Portici, worn out, at nine o'clock in the evening.

In 1783 the pastor Jón Steingrimsson had a ringside seat at Prest Bakki, in southern Iceland, from which to witness the massive eruption of Laki. The eruptive fissure, over 15 miles long, was dotted with 135 craters; 224 square miles of land were covered with lava. The pollution of the waters and the climatic disturbances caused the death of more than 10,000 people and 60 percent of the island's livestock.

With my companions I went to the crevasse. The river of fire had now achieved a size comparable to that of our great rivers during the spring melt. In the middle of this river rocks and blocks of stone rushed and tumbled as if there were enormous wheels swimming there, or things of that type, everything brought to a fiery red. When they struck something hard in their path, in front of them or to the side, or when the rocks collided, making sparks with the blow, flashes and tongues of flame flew here and there, so big that they made an awful spectacle.

I also watched the underground eruption. First the earth swelled up, with a chorus of howls, filled with an uproar that made it explode into pieces, tore it apart, and eviscerated it like when a rabid animal rips something to bits.

Then flames and fire came out of the slightest hole in the lava. Big blocks of stone and sods of turf were thrown into the air to an unspeakable height, from time to time accompanied by great bangs, flashes, jets of sand, and light or dense smoke. Oh what terror it was to contemplate such signs of fury, such divine manifestations!

On the 9th ash was diverted toward the whole of Sida [a region of Iceland], so that the earth was black. On the 10th the same fall of ash continued. On the 11th and 12th there came a great rain and wind; they harassed these ashes and dispersed them so that the soil reappeared. In places such as the Medalland [another region], where, it was learned, there had been no fall of sand and the livestock had survived, a few peasants returned and went as far west as necessary to take shelter with their livestock, although this was of little use. Because when the Lord wants to inflict punishment, nobody can escape His wrath.

On 20 July, the fifth Sunday after Trinity, there was the same overcast weather, with thunderclaps, lightning, and underground grumbling and movement. And as the weather was passable, I went to church, together with everybody who was here in Sida—locals and those who had managed to get here—with the fearful and painful thought that this might well be the last time that one would hold a service there, under the influence of the fear that the moment was approaching when it would be devastated. Thunderclaps and lightning came in quick succession and with such force that everything in the church was lit up and there were echoes in the bells. The ground trembled frequently.

The great distress that then seized us caused me and others to pray to God that, in His mercy, He might not wish to destroy us quickly, nor this house which belonged to Him, so great was His all-powerful strength in the face of our fragility. Like all those present, I remained totally intrepid on the inside; nobody looked as though they wanted to leave or flee before the end of the divine service, although I made it last as long as usual. It was a suitable time to talk to God....

After the service we went to see what progress the fire had made: It had not advanced noticeably since our arrival; it had preferred to spend that time piling up and swelling within the same limits, layer upon layer, there, in the sloping riverbed—and will remain visible there until the end of the world if there are no further changes.

The eruptive fissure of Laki.

The Holtsá and Fjadará [rivers] overflowed the embankments that the new lava had built them, their impetuous breaking waves stifled the fire that was pursuing its course in the riverbed and moving forward and downward; they formed cascades and rushed among the lava flows. This river was so great that it was totally impassable by horses throughout that day, below the monastery.

We then left the church, more joyful than words could say, and thanked God for having protected us and delivered us—and His house—so helpfully. Yes, may all those alive today and those yet unborn who see this all-powerful work or hear about it praise and celebrate His sublime name. From that same day on, the fire did no notable damage in my parish.

Tourists Conquer the Craters

Despite the dangers, erupting volcanoes attract increasing numbers of tourists eager to see beautiful spectacles and experience powerful sensations. Guided visits began on Vesuvius and spread to Etna, and today can be found on volcanoes all over the world.

The Ascent of Vesuvius

What might be called the touristic glory of Vesuvius began practically at the start of the 19th century, and a real industry sprang up which employed coachmen, guides, and even bearers—for the weakest or richest foreigners preferred to reach the volcano's summit not, of course, on their own feet but comfortably seated on a special chair carried by four robust youths. From Naples one normally set off during the night, in a carriage.

Vesuvius could be tackled from three sides: from Resina, San Sebastiano, and Boscotrecase; but the usual route was that from Resina.

At Resina the meeting place was on a square ornamented by a 17th-century fountain called Fontana dei Colli Mozzi; there, in a shop bearing the inscription Ciceroni del Real Vesuvio, one discussed prices; then one mounted a horse or a donkey....

Around 1840 the tariffs were fixed as follows: a night visit with a donkey, 2 ducats and 40 grani; a night visit with a horse, 3 ducats; a daytime visit with a donkey, 1 ducat and 20 grani; a daytime visit with a horse, 1 ducat and 50 grani. But these were just rough prices, which often gave rise to endless disputes; so much so that on 3 September 1846 a prefectorial regulation was issued, with the following text: "When guides are not satisfied with what has been offered for their services, they can insist without, however, asking more than 10 carlins for daytime excursions and 12 for nighttime excursions; this is in addition

Visiting Vesuvius by mule-chair.

to the costs of hiring chairs and the animals used for the transport of visitors, costs which must not exceed 4 ducats per chair with 8 porters, and 8 carlins per mule, horse, and donkey, provided these animals are equipped with saddles and that the saddle is solid and appropriate." Most visitors, of course, preferred to make nighttime excursions to see the reddish lights of Vesuvius.

So the strange cortege of visitors and guides, all preceded by a young boy holding a lamp or torch, began the climb. They traveled along a road flanked by numerous villas and reached the hermitage; naturally, after 1848, that is, after the completion of a proper road leading to the observatory, it was possible to do this part of the journey in a carriage, unless prevented from doing so by lava.

The halt at the hermitage was indispensable for rest and refreshment. While serving his guests, the hermit presented them with a big book whose title page bore the words Album of the Hermitage of Vesuvius, and he asked—even insisted—that each person add his or her signature. This album—or rather these various albums—were quickly transformed into a precious collection of autographs: The names of Goethe, Monti, Byron, Dumas, Malibran, Alfieri, Lamartine, and Flaubert are just a few of the most famous. Many were happy to write little poems or witticisms....

Once past the hermitage, the real climb began, and in this phase of the excursion, the collaboration of the guides, tied to the travelers with ropes, was absolutely indispensable, for there was a constant risk of stumbling, sinking into burning lava, or being exposed to a sudden fall of lapilli. For their part, the guides (and this formed part of the ritual) vied with each other at telling sinister tales to increase the visitors' apprehension.

There is a whole literature on the behavior of the Vesuvius guides. It has been said that, on the pretext of making molds in the lava, they asked to be given a coin and then declared later that they had lost it; it is also said that they indulged in an excess of naive tricks and jokes, like lighting a cigarette by putting it near a burning stone, and so on, but in many cases the complaints cannot have been well founded. In reality, these tough men exercised a real fascination over the female foreign travelers who, seated on their chairs and carried by porters, ended up imagining themselves to be queens....

Be that as it may, once the crater had been reached, any recriminations ceased because the spectacle of the cone on one side and the plain on the other was so intoxicating. It was difficult for the tourists not to succumb to the temptation of setting their impressions down on paper; and if by chance the visitor was a scholar, this was indispensable. This is how, in the 19th century, the fashion spread of writing a personal journal, dated in a romantic way, "at the summit of Vesuvius, at the very moment of the eruption"; some, like Chateaubriand, even claimed to have filled their journals with notes written on the spot, between a fumarole and a lava flow: "Here I am on the top of Vesuvius, writing while seated at the mouth of the volcano, and ready to descend to the bottom of its crater."

Vittorio Paliotti
Il Vesuvio, Una Storia Scottante
1981

Sep.'20.'h 1831

Naturalists on Vesuvius.

Tourists on Vesuvius.

Impressions of Etna

At last I have seen Etna!

For four days and three nights I have trodden the fire-spewing colossus.

At this very moment I am leaving the great laboratory where, in the words of Spallanzani, nature works in secret on its chemical operations.

Having barely escaped the deserts, chasms, gases, sulfurs, ashes, scoria, and lava, I am stunned, intoxicated, choked by sulfurous vapors, filled with volcanic fumes; I'm still shaky on my legs and don't quite know where I am.

In less than ninety-seven hours I have tried everything that can be tried: I have done everything that can be done: I have seen everything that can be seen: I have suffered all that can be suffered.

Fatigue, thirst, terror, the greatest heat, the most intense cold, I have felt them all in turn. Often they all struck me at the same time.

I have trodden the floor of a chasm, which nobody had trodden before me, I have aged five years in five days, and I have worn out two pairs of boots.

But after all, I have seen Etna; and even if I were now to die or be reduced to going barefoot, I can have no regrets either for my footsteps or for my footwear!

However, in view of the state I am in, some rest appears necessary; any man who has just come from where I have been might well hesitate to set off again. So while my bootmaker is working and my poor legs are resting, the reader will find here some remarks that are better than mine.

A. de Gourbillon
Voyage Critique à l'Etna
1820

An Accident on Kirishima in Japan

Until now I have seen nothing, felt nothing, heard nothing. The volcano remains silent; not a sound emerges from the earth; not a tremor has shaken the mountain. As the slope is very steep, I climb with my face almost to the ground. I am about to reach the edge of the crater, I'm touching it…when a terrible detonation is heard. The noise is so immense, it so fills the air that at first I cannot determine its direction. My first movement is to return to my guide who had stayed quite far behind me. I see him, his arms raised, fleeing as fast as his legs will carry him. So I look at the crater: A thick column of white vapors, smoke, and gray ashes is rising into the sky, lined with fiery rocks, lit up by red lights that set it ablaze like lightning. At a glance I calculate the extreme point where this rain of projectiles is going to fall; there can be no illusion—it would require ten minutes, maybe more, to be out of danger, and in a few seconds the ground will be covered with stones and scoria on fire. Fleeing is useless, death is certain. I take out my watch: It is 8:35; in less than a minute it will all be over.

The column rises, climbing to more than a kilometer; it curves outward like a grandiose sheaf, and from all sides there is a fusillade so powerful that it even drowns out the volcano's rumbling. These are incandescent rocks exploding in the air. The sheaf bends and falls; it is a tremendously beautiful moment. I find myself in the middle of a sphere of fire—the sky and earth disappear and all I have before my eyes, above my head, and below me is an immense red veil that rolls, turns, crackles, falls and…a piece of rock hits me on the head. I am sent spinning and sprawl on the ground, face down, with my right side toward the crater. I remain motionless in this position. Why move? If one is to die, what does it matter where, or whether standing or lying down? A shower of stones falls on to my back, striking it like a volley of blows from a staff; a rain of agglomerated ash, big as walnuts, keeps me pinned irresistibly to the earth. Around me are falling incandescent blocks that make deep holes in the ground and cover me with their fragments.…

But I was not to be stoned to death; cremation was to be my fate. The crater began to disgorge a torrent of burning cinders, stones, and incandescent rocks. In a few seconds this river is upon me. I cover my eyes with my hand to protect them and to try to die with less suffering. The torrent of fire passes over my body; I can only breathe burning vapors; the rocks pile up on my right side and slowly compress it; I am suffocating…when, suddenly, this heap, no doubt pushed by a more vigorous block, is sent flying and comes down on my left hip, which it crushes; fragments strike my heel and left hand, which are dreadfully injured…and I find myself standing up, I don't know how. Since death has consented to spare me, I shall try to flee. I leave my hat, smoking, beside my umbrella; I retrieve my watch, stuck to the back of my neck in a clot of blood, and start to descend, slowly, painfully, under the continuing shower of stones, in the midst of blinding smoke, ashes, and fragments of rock that are tumbling and cascading down the flanks of the mountain and rolling between my legs.…

Etna, the funicular on the slope of Vesuvius.

My guide has not reappeared. After I have given them some indications, a few men of the village set off to bring him help if it is not too late. The information they bring back that evening leaves me in no doubt about his unfortunate fate. They have seen him, far off, stretched out on the flank of the mountain, but the violence of the eruption prevented them approaching.

It is only two days later that, during a brief calm spell, a few brave men are able to climb up to get his corpse. The head, separated from the body, had been flung almost twenty feet from it, which seems to indicate that death caught him in full flight without his having a chance to realize it or to suffer. His watch lay beside him, half melted.

Daniel Lièvre
The Volcanoes of Japan
1890

Volcano Stories

From Virgil (70–19 BC) to Malaparte (1898–1957), Italian writers have been unable to resist volcanoes, which loom so large in their land. The subject of hundreds of texts, they have also fascinated authors from other countries—Jules Verne, Victor Hugo, and Mark Twain, to name just a few.

The Phlegraean Fields

The Abbé de Saint-Non tells of his three-year stay in Italy (1759–61). His book, illustrated with hundreds of engravings, is valuable not only as a historical and geographical work but also as a work of art.

One of the most curious and most interesting phenomena for all travelers is the famous Cave of the Dog, so named because this animal is used there every day for experiments with the air, or rather the noxious acid, that continually emerges from this cave's floor to the height of about one and a half feet....

Before examining the nature of this famous cave's murderous vapor, we shall first accompany our traveler there and hear the account of the experiments he witnessed. "It is at ten inches from the ground that there arises, in a distinctive way, the noxious vapor that suffocates every being dipped into it. The first

Lake Agnano and the Cave of the Dog.

experiment I carried out was on a spider that had attached itself to my hat when I entered the cave. I took it, as it was spinning its silk, and put it down in the vapor. At first it made some effort to climb back up its thread; but as I continued to dip it in, its movements relaxed, and soon it became motionless. I took it out of the cave; it returned to life. I put it back in the vapor; it died there completely.

"Next came the usual victim, the dog…. Its master took it by all four paws, and laid it on the ground. At first it moved like any animal whose breathing is constrained and who struggles to recover it; an instant later its lungs tightened, its stomach was drawn in, its eyes bulged and became staring, its tongue was thickened and pale and hung out of its mouth; by the second minute it was motionless. This

state made us fearful for the fate of this poor animal, which would have been irremediably suffocated had it been left there for two more minutes. No sooner was it out of the cave than the natural air caused its lungs to make the same movement as I had noticed when it had been plunged into the vapor; half a minute later it stood up unsteadily; and after a few moments it eagerly ate the bread we gave it, apparently with no memory of what it had just undergone; the door of the cave did not even cause it any kind of fear…each dog could only withstand this ordeal twelve to fifteen times, after which it became dizzy and died in convulsions, like those which die from rabies."

J. C. Richard de Saint-Non,
Voyage Pittoresque ou Description des Royaumes de Naples et de Sicile, 1781–6

Vesuvius

Elisabeth Vigée-Lebrun (1755–1842), a painter noted for her portraits of French queen Marie-Antoinette, emigrated to Italy at the start of the French Revolution.

Now I must tell you of my various expeditions up Vesuvius….

The first time my companions and myself were caught in a frightful storm, accompanied by rain, which resembled the Deluge. We were drenched, but none the less we continued our road toward a portion of the summit, where we could see one of the great streams of lava running at our feet. I seemed to be standing near one of the entrances to the infernal regions, for the stream of fire, which suffocated me, was three miles in circumference. The bad weather on that day prevented our going further, and the smoke and

J. BLAEU Excud.

Sudatorium S. Germani

quantity of cinders which covered us, made the summit of the mountain invisible.... The thunders of heaven and the mountain mingled together continually; the noise was terrific ...[and] as we were precisely under the cloud, we all trembled lest the movement of our party returning should attract the lightning....

Far from being discouraged by my first attempt, a few days afterward I made my second venture up my dear Vesuvius.... The weather was perfect. Before nightfall we were on the mountain, to see the ancient streams of lava and watch the sunset on the sea. The volcano was more furious than ever, and as in the day time no fire can be seen, we watched the showers of cinders and lava pouring out of the crater, and remarked the beautiful hue the setting sun threw over the scene.

We mounted to the Hermitage. The sun set gloriously behind the islands of Ischia and Procida; what a view! Then night came on, and the smoke was transformed into flames, the most beautiful sight imaginable. Tongues of fire darted from the crater, sending out great stones from the mouth, and the earth shook beneath our feet.

Elisabeth Vigée-Lebrun
Souvenirs, 1879

At the start of his career as a writer-diplomat, François-Auguste-René de Chateaubriand (1768–1848) was secretary at the French embassy in Rome. His descriptions of Naples and its region were published later in Travels in Italy.

Jan. 5, 1804
I left Naples this 5th of January, at seven o'clock in the morning, and proceeded to Portici. The sun had dispersed the clouds of night, but the top of Vesuvius is always wrapt in mist. I began my journey up the mountain with a *Cicerone*, who provided two mules, one for me, and another for himself.

At first our ascent was by a tolerably wide road, between two plantations of vines, which were trained upon poplars.

Eruption of Vesuvius on 8 August 1779.

I soon began to feel the cold wintry air, but kept advancing, and at length perceived, a little below the vapours of the middle region, the tops of some trees. They were the elms of the hermitage. The miserable habitations of the vine-dressers were now visible on either side, amidst a rich abundance of *Lachrymae Christi*. In other respects, I observed a parched soil, and naked vines intermixed with pine-trees in the form of an umbrella, some aloes in the hedge, innumerable rolling stones, and not a single bird.

On reaching the first level ground, a naked plain stretched itself before me, and I had also in view the two summits of Vesuvius—on the left the Somma, on the right the present mouth of the volcano. These two heads were enveloped in pale clouds. I proceeded. On one side the Somma falls in, and on the other I could distinguish the hollows made in the cone of the volcano, which I was about to climb. The lava of 1766 and 1769 covered the plain I was then crossing. It was a frightful smoky desert, where the lava, cast out like dross from a forge, displays its whitish scum upon the black ground, exactly resembling dried moss....

The prevailing colour of the gulph is jet black; but Providence, as I have often observed, can impart grace and pleasure even to objects the most revolting. The lava, in some places, is tinged with azure, ultra marine, yellow, and orange. Rocks of granite are warped and twisted by the action of the fire, and bent to their very extremities, so that they exhibit the semblance of the leaves of palms and acanthus. The volcanic matter having cooled on the rocks over which it flowed, many figures are thus formed, such as roses, girandoles, and ribbons. The rocks likewise assume the forms of plants and animals, and imitate the various figures which are to be seen in agates. I particularly noticed, on a bluish rock, a white swan, modelled so perfectly that I could have almost sworn I beheld this beautiful bird sleeping upon a placid lake, its head bent under its wing, and its long neck stretched over its back like a roll of silk....

Pliny perished owing to his desire to contemplate, at a distance, the volcano, in the centre of which I was now tranquilly seated. I saw the abyss smoking around me. I reflected that a few fathoms below me was a gulph of fire. I reflected that the volcano might at once disgorge its entrails, and launch me into the air amidst the rocky fragments by which I was surrounded.

François-Auguste-René de Chateaubriand, *Travels in America and Italy*, 1828

Victor Hugo devoted one of his poems to Vesuvius.

When huge Vesuvius in its torment long,
Threatening has growled its cavernous jaws among,
When its hot lava, like the bubbling wine,
Foaming doth all its monstrous edge incarnadine,
Then is alarm in Naples.
   With dismay,
Wanton and wild her weeping thousands pour,
Convulsive grasp the ground, its rage to stay,
Implore the angry Mount—in vain implore!
For lo! a column tow'ring more and more,
Of smoke and ashes from the burning crest
Shoots like a vulture's neck reared from its airy nest.

Sudden a flash, and from th'enormous den
Th'eruption's lurid mass bursts forth amain,
Bounding in frantic ecstasy. Ah! then
Farewell to Grecian fount and Tuscan fane!
Sails in the bay imbibe the purpling stain,
The while the lava in profusion wide

Flings o'er the mountain's neck its
  showery locks untied.

It comes—it comes! that lava deep and
  rich,
That dower which fertilizes fields and
  fills
New moles upon the waters, bay and
  beach.
Broad sea and clustered isles, one terror
  thrills
As roll the red inexorable rills;
  While Naples trembles in her palaces,
More helpless than the leaves when
  tempests shake the trees.

Prodigious chaos, streets in ashes
  lost,
Dwellings devoured and vomited
  again.
Roofs against neighbour-roof,
  bewildered, tossed.
The waters boiling and the burning
  plain;
While clang the giant steeples as they
  reel,
Unprompted, their own tocsin peal.

Yet 'mid the wreck of cities, and the
  pride
Of the green valleys and the isles laid
  low,
The crash of walls, the tumult waste
  and wide.
O'er sea and land; 'mid all this work
  of woe,
Vesuvius still, though close its crater-
  glow,
Forgetful spares—Heaven wills that it
  should spare,
The lonely cell where kneels an aged
  priest in prayer.

Victor Hugo
The Poetical Works
translated by various authors, 1885

*"Vesuvius Awakes for Joy at Being
Reunited with His Old Friends from
America." This was, on 19 March 1944,
the headline of the newspaper* Stars and
Stripes *printed in Naples by the
American high command of the 5th
Army, newly arrived in the Neapolitan
countryside. A few days later, the volcanic
bombs of Vesuvius destroyed almost all the
allied military planes at Poggiomarina!
The novelist Curzio Malaparte, a fiery
narrator, devoted a chapter of his book* La
Pelle *to the eruption of Vesuvius in 1944.
He tells of both real events such as the
destruction of several villages and partly
imaginary ones such as the panic of the
Neapolitans and Americans.*

The sky, torn to the east by an immense
wound, was bleeding, and the blood
dyed the sea red. The horizon collapsed
in an abyss of fire. Shaken by profound
shocks, the earth trembled, the houses
wobbled on their foundations, and one
could already hear the dull noise of tiles
and plaster detaching themselves from
the roofs and cornices of the terraces
and hitting the road—precursory signs
of a universal disaster. A sinister
crackling spread through the air, a
cracking of broken, crushed bones. And
dominating the din, above all the
weeping, above the people howling
with terror and running here and there,
staggering in the streets like a blind
man, there rose a terrible cry that
ripped the sky apart.
  Vesuvius howled into the night,
spitting out blood and fire. Since the
day when Herculaneum and Pompeii
were buried alive in their tomb of ash
and stones, such a horrible voice had
never been heard in the sky. A gigantic
tree of fire shot up very high, out of the
volcano's mouth. It was an immense

and marvelous column of smoke and flames that sprang up into the firmament until it seemed to touch the pale stars. On the slopes of Vesuvius, rivers of lava flowed toward the villages scattered through the green of the vineyards....

Torrents of mud lazily descended from the slopes of Monte Somma, twisting around on themselves like black serpents, and where they hurled themselves into the rivers of lava, high clouds of purple vapor arose and a horrible hissing reached us, just like the cry of red-hot iron when it is plunged into water.

An immense black cloud, like the sac of the cuttlefish (in fact this cloud bears the name *seccia* [meaning cuttlefish] in Neapolitan), swollen with ash and incandescent stones, tore itself with great difficulty from the summit of Vesuvius and, propelled by the wind which, fortunately for Naples, blew from the northwest, it dragged itself through the sky towards Castellammare di Stabia. The noise made by this black cloud, swollen with stones, as it rolled through the sky, resembled the racket of a cart loaded with rocks that is traveling along a broken-up road....

Vesuvius erupting on 23 March 1944.

The American soldiers, mixed in with this crowd that carried them this way and that in its wake, pushing and striking them like Dante's tempest, also seemed to be gripped by an ancient terror and fury. Their faces were grimy with sweat and ash, their uniforms in tatters. They too were now beaten men, no longer free: not the proud victors but the wretched defeated, at the mercy of nature's blind fury; they too were reduced to ashes in the depths of their souls by the fire that was burning heaven and earth.

After wandering for a long time, we finally emerged on to the huge square, dominated by the Angevin castle, that opens in front of the port. And there, facing us, we saw Vesuvius wrapped in its purple robe. This spectral Caesar with a dog's head, sitting on his throne of lava and ash, pierced the sky, his forehead crowned with lava, and barked horribly. The tree of fire that emerged from his jaws plunged deeply into the celestial vault and disappeared in the supreme abysses. Rivers of blood sprang from his gaping red throat, and the earth, sky, and sea shuddered.

The crowd that was rushing into the square had flat, shining faces, cracking open with white and black shadows, like in a photograph taken by magnesium flare. Everything that is motionless, fixed, cruel in a photograph could be seen in these haggard, staring eyes, in these tense faces, in the facades of the houses, and almost in the gestures. The light of the fire struck the walls, lit the gutters and the cornices of the terraces. And against the sky of blood, its dark color bordering on violet, these red gums edging the roofs created haunting contrasts. Groups of people headed for the sea, emerging from the hundred alleys that converged on the square from all directions, and walked with their faces turned toward the black clouds, swollen with flaming fragments, that rolled in the sky above the sea, toward the incandescent stones that streaked through the dirty air, whistling like comets....

In April 1944, after having shaken the earth horribly for several days and vomited torrents of fire, Vesuvius went out. It did not go out little by little, but suddenly. Its forehead enveloped in a shroud of clouds, it uttered a great cry and, suddenly, the coldness of death petrified its veins of fire. The god of Naples, the totem of the Neapolitan people, was dead. An immense veil of black crepe came down over the city, the sea, and Posilipo. In the streets, people walked on tiptoe, speaking in hushed tones, as if fearing to awaken the dead....

And if, sometimes, the fire of sunset, the silvery reflection of the moon, or a ray from the sunrise seemed to inflame the white ghost of the volcano, a sharp cry, like that of a woman in labor, arose from the town. Everyone went to their windows, rushed into the street, embraced each other while weeping for joy, carried away by the hope that life had miraculously returned to the volcano's dried-up veins, and that this bloody note of the setting sun, this reflection of the moon, or this timid light of dawn was the herald of the resurrection of Vesuvius, of that dead god whose naked corpse encumbered the sad sky of Naples. But disappointment and rage quickly followed this hope; tears dried, and the crowd, loosing their hands that had been joined in prayer, raised threatening fists or jeered at the volcano, mixing supplications and complaints with insults: "Have pity on us, accursed mountain! Son of a whore, have pity on us!"

Curzio Malaparte
La Pelle, 1949

Etna

According to Virgil, the volcano is the abode of the gods.

Meanwhile the wind falls with sundown; and weary and ignorant of the way we glide down on to the Cyclopes' coast. There lies a harbour large and unstirred by the winds' entrance; but nigh it Aetna thunders awfully in wrack, and ever and again hurls a black cloud into the sky, smoking with boiling pitch and embers white hot, and heaves balls of flame flickering up to the stars: ever and again vomits out on high crags from the torn entrails of the mountain, tosses up masses of molten rock with a groan, and boils forth from the bottom. Rumour is that this mass weighs down the body of Enceladus, half-consumed by the thunderbolt, and mighty Aetna laid over him suspires the flame that bursts from her furnaces; and so often as he changes his weary side, all Trinacria shudders and moans, veiling the sky in smoke. That night we spend in cover of the forest among portentous horrors, and see not from what source the noise comes. For neither did the stars show their fires, nor was the vault of constellated sky clear; but vapours blotted heaven, and the moon was held in a storm-cloud through dead of night.

Virgil
The Aeneid, Book III
translated by J. W. Mackail, 1885

Alexandre Dumas (1802–70) spent much time in Italy; he was even, for four years, director of the Archaeological Museum of Naples and the excavations of Pompeii. He knew Vesuvius as well as Etna, which he described in Le Spéronare, *an account of his voyage to Sicily.*

After dinner, Mr. Gemellaro inquired about the precautions we had taken for climbing up Etna. We replied that our precautions were limited to buying a bottle of rum and cooking two or three chickens. Mr. Gemellaro then looked at our clothing and, seeing Jadin with his velvet and me with my cloth jacket, he asked us with a shudder if we did not have overcoats or cloaks. We replied that for the moment we possessed only what was on our backs.

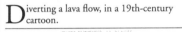 Diverting a lava flow, in a 19th-century cartoon.

"Typical Frenchmen," murmured Mr. Gemellaro, getting up; "you would not catch a German or an Englishman setting off like that. Wait, wait." And he went to fetch us two enormous coats with hoods....

We were about a third of the way up, we had taken almost half an hour to climb four hundred feet; the east was becoming lighter and lighter; the fear of not reaching the top of the cone in time to see the sunrise restored all our energy, and we set off with fresh zeal, without stopping to look at the immense horizon which, with every step, broadened beneath our feet; but the more we advanced, the greater the difficulties: With every step the slope became steeper, the earth more friable, and the air thinner. Soon, to our right, we began to hear underground roaring that attracted our attention; our guide walked ahead of us and led us to a fissure from which there emerged, with great noise and driven by an interior draft, a thick sulfurous smoke. As we approached the edge of this cleft, we saw, at a depth we could not measure, a red, liquid, incandescent bottom; and when we struck the earth with our feet, it resonated far off like a drum. Fortunately, the earth was perfectly calm, because, if the wind had driven this smoke toward us, it would have suffocated us....

After a halt of several minutes at the edge of this furnace, we set off again, climbing obliquely, to make things easier; I began to have a ringing in my head, as if blood were going to come out of my ears, and the air, which was getting less and less breathable, made me pant as if I were going to stop breathing altogether. I wanted to lie down to rest a little, but the earth was

exhaling such a smell of sulfur that I had to give up the notion. I then had the idea of placing my tie over my mouth, and breathing through its cloth; this soothed me.

However, little by little, we had done three quarters of the climb, and we saw the mountain's summit only a few hundred feet above our heads. We made a final effort, and half upright, half on all fours, we recommenced the ascent of this short distance, not daring to look below for fear of our heads turning, so steep was the slope. Finally Jadin, who was a few paces ahead of me, uttered a triumphant shout: He had arrived and found himself before the crater; a few seconds later I was beside him. We found ourselves literally between two abysses.

Once we had reached there, and having no further need to make any violent movements, we began to breathe more easily; moreover, the spectacle before our eyes was so thrilling that it lessened our discomfort, however great.

We were face to face with the crater, an immense hole eight miles around and nine hundred feet deep; the walls of this cavity were covered from top to bottom in scarified material, sulfur, and alum; at the bottom, as far as we could see from that distance, there was some kind of boiling material, and from this chasm there arose a fine, tortuous smoke, like a gigantic serpent standing upright on its tail. The edges of the crater were irregular in cut, and of differing height. We were on one of the highest points.

Our guide...invited us to move some twenty feet away from the crater, to avoid any accidents, and to look around us....

For three quarters of an hour the spectacle merely grew in magnificence. I have seen the sun rise over the Rigi and the Faulhorn, those two Swiss titans, but nothing can compare with what one sees from the top of Etna. Calabria, from Pizzo to the Capo delle Armi, the straits from Scylla to Reggio, the Tyrrhenian Sea and the Ionian Sea; to the left, the Aeolian Islands, which seem to be within reach; to the right, Malta, which floats on the horizon like a light mist; around one is the whole of Sicily… finally, the immense crater, roaring, full of flames and smoke; heaven above one's head, hell beneath one's feet: Such a spectacle made us forget everything, fatigue, danger, suffering. My admiration was total, without limits, in good faith, with the eyes of my body and the eyes of my soul. I had never before seen God so close and, consequently, so great.

Alexandre Dumas
Le Spéronare, 1842

From Sneffels to Stromboli: In the Bowels of a Volcano

In A Journey to the Centre of the Earth *by Jules Verne (1828–1905), Professor Lidenbrock and his companions descend into an Icelandic crater and are ejected through Stromboli. Although the famous writer was sometimes fifty years ahead of his time in imagining some of the most astonishing conquests of science, his journey beneath the earth unfortunately still remains impossible.*

The crater of Mount Sneffels represented an inverted cone, the gaping orifice apparently half a mile across; the depth indefinite feet.

The descent into the crater.

Conceive what this *hole* must have been like when full of flame and thunder and lightning. The bottom of the funnel-shaped hollow was about five hundred feet in circumference, by which it will be seen that the slope from the summit to the bottom was very gradual, and we were therefore clearly able to get there without much fatigue or difficulty. Involuntarily, I compared this crater to an enormous loaded cannon; and the comparison terrified me.

"To descend into the interior of a cannon," I thought to myself, "when perhaps it is loaded, and will go off at the least shock, is the act of a madman."…

The descent then commenced in the following order: Hans went first, my uncle followed, and I went last. Our progress was made in profound silence—a silence troubled only by the fall of the pieces of rock.... The heat still remained at quite a supportable degree. With an involuntary shudder, I reflected on what the heat must have been when the volcano of Sneffels was pouring its smoke, flames, and streams of boiling lava—all of which must have come up by the road we were now following. I could imagine the torrents of hot seething stone darting on, bubbling up with accompaniments of smoke, steam, and sulphurous stench!

"Only to think of the consequences," I mused, "if the old volcano were once more to set to work."...

"We are going upwards."

"My dear uncle, what can you mean?" was my half delirious reply.

"Yes, I tell you we are ascending rapidly. Our downward journey is quite checked."

I held out my hand, and, after some little difficulty, succeeded in touching the wall. My hand was in an instant covered with blood. The skin was torn from the flesh. We were ascending with extraordinary rapidity....

And yet, as we progressed, the temperature increased in the most extraordinary degree, and I began to feel as if I were bathed in a hot and burning atmosphere.... I could only compare it to the hot vapour from an iron foundry, when the liquid iron is in a state of ebullition and runs over....

"Are we ascending to a living fire?" I cried; when, to my horror and astonishment, the heat became greater than before.

"No, no," said my uncle, "it is simply impossible, quite impossible."

"And yet," said I, touching the side of the shaft with my naked hand, "this

Above and opposite: Illustrations from Jules Verne's *A Journey to the Centre of the Earth*.

wall is literally burning."

At this moment, feeling as I did that the sides of this extraordinary well were red hot, I plunged my hands into the water to cool them. I drew them back with a cry of despair.

"The water is boiling!" I cried....

"Do you not...recognise all the well-known symptoms—"

"Of an earthquake? By no means. I am expecting something far more important."

"My brain is strained beyond endurance—what, what do you mean?" I cried.

"An eruption...."

"An eruption," I gasped. "We are, then, in the volcanic shaft of a crater in full action and vigour."...

"What!" cried I, in the height of my

exasperation, "we are on the way to an eruption, are we? Fatality has cast us into a well of burning and boiling lava, of rocks on fire, of boiling water, in a word, filled with every kind of eruptive matter? We are about to be expelled, thrown up, vomited, spit out of the interior of the earth…with huge blocks of granite, with showers of cinders and scoria, in a wild whirlwind of flame, and you say—the most fortunate thing which could happen to us."

"Yes," replied the Professor, looking at me calmly from under his spectacles, "it is the only chance which remains to us of ever escaping from the interior of the earth to the light of day."…

An enormous force [was] hoisting us upwards with irresistible power.

But though we were approaching the light of day, to what fearful dangers were we about to be exposed?

Instant death appeared the only fate which we could expect or contemplate.

Soon a dim, sepulchral light penetrated the vertical gallery, which became wider and wider. I could make out to the right and left long dark corridors like immense tunnels, from which awful and horrid vapours poured out. Tongues of fire, sparkling and crackling, appeared about to lick us up.

The hour had come!

"Look, uncle, look!" I cried.

"Well, what you see are the great sulphurous flames. Nothing more common in connection with an eruption."

"But if they lap us round!" I angrily replied.

"They will not lap us round," was his quiet and serene answer.

"But it will be all the same in the end if they stifle us," I cried.

"We shall not be stifled. The gallery is rapidly becoming wider and wider, and if it be necessary, we will presently leave the raft and take refuge in some fissure in the rock."

"But the water, the water, which is continually ascending!" I despairingly replied.

"There is no longer any water…," he answered, "but a kind of lava paste, which is heaving us up, in company with itself, to the mouth of the crater."

In truth, the liquid column of water had wholly disappeared to give place to dense masses of boiling eruptive matter. The temperature was becoming utterly insupportable.…

Towards eight o'clock in the morning a new incident startled us. The ascensional movement suddenly ceased. The raft became still and motionless.

"What is the matter now?" I said, querulously, very much startled by this change.

"A simple halt," replied my uncle.

"Is the eruption about to fail?" I asked.

"I hope not."…

"Good," said my uncle, observing the hour, "in ten minutes we shall start again."

"In ten minutes?"

"Yes—precisely. We have to do with a volcano, the eruption of which is intermittent. We are compelled to breathe just as it does."…

I have…kept no account of what followed for many hours. I have a vague…remembrance of continual detonations, of the shaking of the huge granitic mass, and of the raft going round like a spinning-top. It floated on the stream of hot lava, amidst a falling cloud of cinders. The huge flames roaring, wrapped us around.…

When I opened my eyes I felt the

hand of the guide clutching me firmly by the belt. With his other hand he supported my uncle. I was not grievously wounded, but bruised all over in the most remarkable manner.

After a moment I looked around, and found that I was lying down on the slope of a mountain not two yards from a yawning gulf into which I should have fallen had I made the slightest false step. Hans had saved me from death, while I rolled insensible on the flanks of the crater....

"Look, look, my boy," said the Professor, as dogmatically as usual.

Right above our heads, at a great height, opened the crater of a volcano from which escaped, from one quarter of an hour to the other, with a very loud explosion, a lofty jet of flame mingled with pumice stone, cinders, and lava. I could feel the convulsions of nature in the mountain, which breathed like a huge whale, throwing up from time to time fire and air through its enormous vents.

Below, and floating along a slope of considerable angularity, the stream of eruptive matter spread away to a depth which did not give the volcano a height of three hundred fathoms.

Its base disappeared in a perfect forest of green trees, among which I perceived olives, fig trees, and vines loaded with rich grapes....

Stromboli! What effect on the imagination did these few words produce! We were in the centre of the Mediterranean; amidst the Eastern archipelago of mythological memory; in the ancient Strongylos, where Aeolus kept the wind and the tempest chained up. And those blue mountains, which rose towards the rising of the sun, were the mountains of Calabria.

And that mighty volcano which rose on the southern horizon was Etna, the fierce and celebrated Etna!

"Stromboli! Stromboli!" I repeated to myself.

Jules Verne
A Journey to the Centre of the Earth
English edition
1872

The summit of Stromboli.

The Lava Lake of Kilauea

Mark Twain (1835–1910) was interested in volcanoes. Vesuvius, in his view, was a mere "toy, a child's volcano" compared to the crater of Kilauea in Hawaii.

I suppose that any one of nature's most celebrated wonders will always look rather insignificant to a visitor at first sight, but on a better acquaintance will swell and stretch out and spread abroad, until it finally grows clear beyond his grasp—becomes too stupendous for his comprehension....

After a hearty supper we waited until it was thoroughly dark and then started to the crater. The first glance in that direction revealed a scene of wild beauty. There was a heavy fog over the crater and it was splendidly illuminated by the glare from the fires below. The illumination was two miles wide and a mile high, perhaps; and if you ever, on a dark night and at a distance, beheld the light from thirty or forty blocks of distant buildings all on fire at once, reflected strongly against overhanging clouds, you can form a fair idea of what this looked like.

Arrived at the little thatched lookout house, we rested our elbows on the railing in front and looked abroad over the wide crater and down over the sheer precipice at the seething fires beneath us.... I turned to see the effect on the balance of the company and found the reddest-faced set of men I almost ever saw. In the strong light every countenance glowed like red-hot iron, every shoulder was suffused with crimson and shaded rearward into dingy shapeless obscurity! The place below looked like the infernal regions and these men like half-cooled devils just come up on a furlough....

The greater part of the vast floor of the desert under us was as black as ink, and apparently smooth and level; but over a mile square of it was ringed and streaked and striped with a thousand branching streams of liquid and gorgeously brilliant fire! It looked like a colossal railroad map of the State of Massachusetts done in chain lightning on a midnight sky. Imagine it— imagine a coal-black sky shivered into a tangled network of angry fire!

Here and there were gleaming holes twenty feet in diameter, broken in the dark crust, and in them the melted lava—the color a dazzling white just tinged with yellow—was boiling and surging furiously; and from these holes branched numberless bright torrents in many directions, like the "spokes" of a lady's fan, and kept a tolerably straight course for a while and then swept round in huge rainbow curves, or made a long succession of sharp worm-fence angles, which looked precisely like the fiercest jagged lightning. These streams met other streams, and they mingled with and crossed and recrossed each other in every conceivable direction, like skate tracks on a popular skating ground. Sometimes streams twenty or thirty feet wide flowed from the holes to some distance without dividing— and through the opera glasses we could see that they ran down small, steep hills and were genuine cataracts of fire, white at their source, but soon cooling and turning to the richest red, grained with alternate lines of black and gold. Every now and then masses of the dark crust broke away and floated slowly down these streams like rafts down a river. Occasionally the molten lava flowing under the superincumbent crust broke through—split a dazzling streak, from five hundred to a thous and feet long, like a sudden flash of lightning, and then acre after acre of the cold lava parted into fragments, turned up edgewise like cakes of ice when a great river breaks up, plunged downward and were swallowed in the crimson cauldron. Then the wide expanse of the "thaw" maintained a ruddy glow for a while, but shortly cooled and became black and level again....

The little fountains scattered about looked very beautiful. They boiled, and coughed, and spluttered, and discharged sprays of stringy red fire—of about the consistency of mush, for instance—from ten to fifteen feet into the air....

I forgot to say that the noise made by the bubbling lava is not great, heard as we heard it from our lofty perch. It makes three distinct sounds—a rushing, a hissing, and a coughing or puffing sound; and if you stand on the brink and close your eyes it is no trick at all to imagine that you are sweeping down a river on a large low-pressure steamer, and that you hear the hissing of the steam about her boilers, the puffing from her escape pipes, and the churning rush of the water abaft her wheels. The smell of sulphur is strong, but not unpleasant to a sinner.

We left the lookout house at ten o'clock in a half-cooked condition, because of the heat from Pele's furnaces, and wrapping up in blankets (for the night was cold) returned to the hotel. After we got out in the dark we had another fine spectacle. A colossal column of cloud towered to a great height in the air immediately above the crater, and the outer swell of every one of its vast folds was dyed with a rich crimson luster, which was subdued to a pale rose tint in the depressions between. It glowed like a muffled torch and stretched upward to a dizzy height toward the zenith. I thought it just possible that its like had not been seen since the children of Israel wandered on their long march through the desert so many centuries ago over a path illuminated by the mysterious "pillar of fire." And I was sure that I now had a vivid conception of what the majestic "pillar of fire" was like, which almost amounted to a revelation.

Mark Twain
Letters from Hawaii, 1872

The lava lake of Kilauea, Hawaii.

Observing Ash Flows

Ash flows, or nuées ardentes, have fascinated scientists for centuries. One classic description was made by French mineralogist Alfred Lacroix, who called them "dense clouds of high temperature, which, on skimming over the ground… spread their ravages far and wide, burning and suffocating living beings, destroying the vegetation in their path."

During the terrible eruption of Vesuvius in 1631, witnesses spoke of "torrents of incandescent ashes" and of "clouds of blazing smoke streaked with lightning." They noted that the houses of some villages were covered with ash, smashed in, blown down, and surrounded by stones and the remains of tattered trees. The destructive streams advanced so quickly "that a father who was holding his two children in his arms saw them carried off while he remained alive."

At Torre del Greco the victims seemed to be asleep, with their clothing intact and all their "internal organs burned." All these effects are typical

Explosion at sea at Capelinhos, Azores, in 1957.

of the destructive power of ash flows.

In the Azores witnesses to the eruptions of São Jorge in 1580 and 1808 also refer to these volcanic phenomena. The activity of 1808 was described by an eyewitness, Father João Inacio Da Silveira, priest of a nearby village. He was the first to use the term *ardente nuvem* for ash flow, the Portuguese equivalent of *nuée ardente*.

"On 17 May…a typhoon of fire emerged from the volcano and crossed the cultivated fields…forming a powerful ash flow that advanced as far as below the church, burning more than thirty people…. Some had flesh hanging off their hands and feet, others were so blistered and blackened that they were unrecognizable, while others had their legs broken or were drawing their last breath…. The ash flows…were filled with dust…which weighed them down and made them crawl along the ground, down the slopes to the sea. They had tremendous lethal power; the entry of the slightest part of these clouds into the lungs brought death."

Naturalist Theodore Wolf reported that, according to the Indians living at the foot of Cotopaxi in Ecuador, the volcano began "boiling" and "effervescing" in 1877. A black mass emerged from the crater, incandescent by night, smoking and full of vapor, and spilled over on all sides, pouring down the cone's flanks at great speed. It was just like the "froth of a pan of rice overflowing on to the fire." All this "boiling glowing mass" came out in a quarter of an hour; the noise it made increased as it descended, it melted the ice and caused gigantic mud flows.

The first volcanologists to get a

Ferdinand-André Fouqué (1828–1904), mentor and father-in-law of Alfred Lacroix, introduced the term *nuée ardente* to the scientific literature.

close look at the ash flows of Mount Pelée were Tempest Anderson and John Flett, on the evening of 9 July 1902, when they were on a boat off Saint-Pierre, Martinique. They described the sight in *Report on the Eruptions of the Soufrière, in St. Vincent, in 1902, and on a Visit to Montagne Pelée in Martinique,* which was published in 1903:

"Suddenly a great yellow or reddish glare lit up the whole cloud mass that veiled the summit…. Then in an instant a red-hot avalanche rose from the cleft in the hillside and poured over the mountain slopes right down to the sea. It was dull red, and in it were brighter streaks, which we thought were large stones, as they seemed to give off tails of yellow sparks…. The main mass of the avalanche was a darker red, and its surface was billowy like a cascade in a mountain brook. Its velocity was

The ruins of Saint-Pierre, Martinique, after the 1902 eruption of Mount Pelée.

tremendous…. The red glow faded… and…we now saw, rushing forward over the sea, a great rounded, boiling cloud…filled with lightnings. It came straight out of the avalanche…and as it advanced it visibly swelled…. The cloud was black, dense, solid, and opaque…like a mass of ink. It was globular as seen end on, very perfectly rounded, but covered with innumerable minor excrescences…. They shot out, swelled, and multiplied till the whole surface seemed boiling; one had hardly time to form before another sprung up at its side; but they were directed mostly to the front and fewer at the margins, so that their effect was that the cloud drove onward without expanding laterally to any great extent."

They estimated that it was almost two miles wide and almost a mile high. Fortunately, while still about a mile distant from the two volcanologists the cloud lost its energy and speed

and dispersed; otherwise Anderson and Flett could never have described what they saw!

Between October 1902 and March 1903 Lacroix observed numerous ash flows on Mount Pelée; he photographed those of 16 December and 25 January and described them in minute detail: "The emergence of an ash flow was usually accompanied by a dull rumbling, caused by the creation of the provisional opening through which the emission was to take place, and by the collapse of the solid material of the carapace of the dome….

"The moment it appeared, the flow looked like a compact mass of small size, but immediately it began to swell, taking the form of a mammillated bud…lined with numerous convolutions with deep meanders, which grew ceaselessly [and which] unceasingly rolled over each other, expanding each time; consequently the volume of the flow increased the more it advanced, and soon it constituted a vertical wall, sometimes reaching 13,000 feet in height and advancing with a terrifying majesty.... The ash flows that went to the sea (at speeds varying between 35 and 80 feet per second), at almost 2 miles from the coast, where the slopes became gentle, sometimes clearly slowed down and almost stopped.... They comprise a thorough mix...of solid materials held in suspension in water vapor and gases.... The temperature of ash flows did not exceed 1100° C when they left the crater. After a journey of nearly 4 miles it was still more than 200°."

During the 1929 eruption of Mount Pelée, an even more intrepid American volcanologist, Frank Perret, built himself a hut on the volcano's heights and observed, sometimes from scarcely 10 feet away, dozens of ash flows pouring down in front of him.

One of them even enveloped him in its cloud, but he survived.

He wrote while observing the dome of pasty lava from which the ash flows sprang:

"The first thing one saw...was a mass advancing obliquely, developing in volume with such speed that it seemed it must fill the whole sky in a moment or two, but suddenly the cloud ceased its rapid vertical expansion and spread horizontally...along the mountain slope and, at the same moment, climbed upward in convolutions of dust and ash in the shape of a cauliflower.

"These convolutions climbed above a mass of incandescent matter that was flowing, advancing with incredible movements of rolling and spurting that, at the front, resembled jets of smoke and reminded one of charging lions."

Since then, volcanologists all over the world have studied these terrible ash flows which, in the last five hundred years, have caused the death of 60,000 people.

Maurice Krafft

A sh flow of Augustine, Alaska, in August 1986.

The Birth of Volcanoes

The appearance of a new volcano is quite a rare phenomenon. But while only a few in a century are born on land, probably dozens are born on the ocean floor. The first gurglings of newborn volcanoes have sometimes been observed, and they often make a good story.

Parícutin

It arose in Mexico, in the middle of a field in Michoacán; this field had always contained a hole, about 15 feet in diameter, into which its owner, Dionisio Pulido, used to throw rubbish, never managing to fill it up. Starting on 5 February 1943, the inhabitants of the village of Parícutin and those of the town of San Juan Parangaricutiro, located about 1 and 3 miles away, felt the ground vibrate and heard strange underground rumblings which grew increasingly louder. In a single day, 19 February, there was a succession of 300 shocks!

The next day, the 20th, at about 4 PM, Dionisio Pulido was surprised to hear loud rumbles while he was preparing his field for sowing. He then saw a crack, 20 inches deep, that passed through his field's famous hole. Then the trees began to tremble, and he saw the earth rise up along the now-gaping fissure, from which smoke was escaping with a hiss, while a nauseating smell of sulfur was spreading. Panic-stricken, he returned to Parícutin. The next day, Pulido went back to his field and discovered a cone of ash and cinders over 30 feet high exploding furiously; it grew rapidly, and by midday was already 150 feet high. After a week the new volcano, Parícutin, stood about 500 feet above the field. Explosions could be heard 300 miles away; it spat ashes and blocks of lava up to 3200 feet into the air. One year later it reached its final size: 1100 feet. It covered Pulido's land completely.

In July 1944, a lava flow came out of

Volcanic eruption at Pozzuoli.

the cone and, having traveled 6 miles in 8 months, entered San Juan. At the end of September of that same year, the village of Parícutin, buried under ashes and abandoned for a year, was flattened by the flows. Dionisio Pulido sold his grumbling and spitting volcano to an artist, Doctor Atl, who was passionately fond of volcanoes and would eventually complete 11,000 drawings and 1000 paintings of the volcano.

Parícutin was to thunder and vomit its lava for nine years and twelve days!

A Volcanic Piston

By coincidence, in the same year that Parícutin was born, another volcano appeared in Japan, in southern Hokkaido. Starting on 24 December 1943 seismic shocks intensified in the region of the volcano Usu. At the end of January 1944 the ground rose progressively. Roads, houses, and irrigation canals in the surrounding area were split. Springs dried up in the zone of the swelling and overflowed in neighboring areas. Then the center of the swelling, which was 2 miles in diameter, became fixed very close to the village of Fukaba. In mid-June the ground had risen more than 160 feet and the seismic shocks were increasing, until they reached 250 per day! Fukaba was the summit of a gigantic piston that kept rising unceasingly.

On 23 June, phreatic explosions of mud and sand broke out, and a crater 160 feet in diameter was born; it was to remain active for 3 months. On 2 July a tremendous explosion threw up 2 million tons of ash caused by the pulverization of old rocks; it inflicted great damage on crops and forests and forced the inhabitants of Fukaba, the "elevator village," to abandon their

The village of Parícutin in 1943, before its destruction by the volcano.

homes. The ground continued to rise, forming a hill which, by October, was 500 feet high! It was called Showa-Shinzan ("new mountain of the Showa era"). As a result of the extent of the deformation, the railway track had to be moved and the nearby river was transformed into a lake.

Finally, on 1 November 1944, an incandescent dome of very pasty lava, 1000° C and nearly 1000 feet in diameter, pierced the swelling and grew until September 1945, when it towered 350 feet over the peak of Showa-Shinzan and 900 feet over the pre-1943 ground level. Mr. Mimatsu, the postmaster of Sobetsu, a town about a mile from the monster, regularly drew the volcano's changing silhouette, thus enabling Japanese volcanologists to study the speed of the dome's growth, which occurred in fits and starts.

Maurice Krafft
Questions for a Volcanologist, 1981

The Gigantic Explosion of Mount Saint Helens

Two volcanic catastrophes marked the 1980s—the awakening in 1980 of Mount Saint Helens, in the northwestern United States, and in 1985 that of Nevado del Ruiz, in Colombia. The activity of Mount Saint Helens especially benefited science, because, for the first time, volcanologists were able to observe all the phases of a gigantic explosive cataclysm.

Mount Saint Helens, which had been dormant since 1857, became active in late March 1980 with a swarm of earthquakes.... Eruptions began on March 27 with a short crater-forming event.... The climactic eruption began at 8:32 AM on May 18, probably triggered by an earthquake of magnitude 5 that caused failure of the bulging north flank.... This failure rapidly unloaded the volcanic edifice, and probably caused the water in its hydrothermal system to flash to steam, initiating a series of...hydrothermal blasts that devastated an area of 230 square miles. These events in turn triggered a 9-hour...magmatic eruption that drove a Plinian column more than 12 miles high, producing ash fallout for more than 930 miles to the east as well as pumiceous ash flows on the volcano's north flank. Catastrophic mudflows and floods were generated from rapid melting of snow and ice and water....

The earthquake caused avalanching from the walls of the crater and... triggered a sudden instability of the north flank.... A small, dark, ash-rich

Trees flattened by the blast from Mount Saint Helens in 1980.

eruption plume rose directly from the base of the scarp and another from the summit crater rose to heights of about 650 feet. As virtually the entire upper north flank…became a massive debris avalanche, a blast broke through the remainder of the flank…and devastated an area nearly 20 miles from west to east and more than 12 miles northward from the former summit. In an inner zone extending nearly 6 miles from the summit…no trees remained. Beyond, nearly to the limit of the blast, all standing trees were blown to the ground, and at the blast's outer limit the trees were left standing but thoroughly seared.…The bulk of the avalanche…turned westward down the valley of the North Fork Toutle River to form a craggy…deposit, part of which crossed the ridge to the north, but most of which flowed as far as 14 miles down the North Toutle. The total volume of the avalanche in place is about .67 cubic miles, and its length makes it one of the largest on record.…

The initial events of the eruption… caused most of the casualties and destruction in the immediate region of the volcano. However, within a few minutes a Plinian eruption column began to rise from the position of the former summit crater and within less than 10 minutes had risen to a height of more than 12 miles. Ash from this eruption cloud was rapidly blown east-northeastward, producing lightning and starting hundreds of small forest fires, causing darkness eastward for more than 120 miles, and depositing ash for many hundreds of miles. Major ash falls occurred as far east as central Montana, and ash fell visibly as far eastward as the Great Plains…more than 900 miles away.… The eruptive crater, along with

Plinian plume (or column) from Mount Saint Helens, 22 July 1980.

the upper 900 feet of the cone that was entirely removed by the initial slide and blast, formed a great amphitheater.…

The Plinian phase of the eruption continued vigorously for 9 hours.… The hot blast deposits, the avalanche, and these ash flows were frequently disrupted…by large secondary steam-blast eruptions that formed craters as large as 65 feet across and drove columns of ash to heights as great as 6500 feet above the surface.… The Plinian eruption began to decrease in intensity at about 17:30 on May 18.… Weak steam and ash eruptions continued intermittently for about a week.

Robert L. Christiansen and Donald W. Peterson, *The 1980 Eruptions of Mount Saint Helens, Washington,* 1981

Volcanism and Plate Tectonics

The theory of plate tectonics, first described twenty years ago, was as revolutionary to the earth sciences as Einstein's theory of relativity was to physics. Plate tectonics enabled volcanologists to understand, among other things, the distribution of volcanoes on the surface of the globe and the types of magma they eject. The following passage is taken from a publication of the Institute of Global Physics in Paris.

Volcanoes are constructed by the accumulation of lava, or partially degassed magma, at particular points on the earth's surface. The origin of magma, a mixture of silicate liquids at high temperature that is often rich in dissolved gases, is sought in our planet's internal mechanisms and is currently understood using plate tectonics.

The Earth's Internal Structure

The earth's internal structure can be subdivided, from the surface to the center, into three concentric parts that are clearly differentiated through their physical and chemical properties:
• the lithosphere, an average of 40 to 60 miles thick, whose upper part comprises the terrestrial crust (oceanic or continental);
• the mantle, the greatest in volume (83 percent), some 1750 miles thick; and
• the core, about 2200 miles in radius, comprising an external fluid envelope and a solid heart, the seed.

One can also differentiate the

Diagram showing the three types of volcanism.

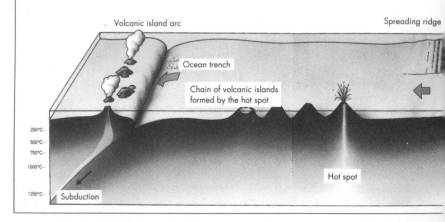

asthenosphere, a plastic layer about 370 miles thick, located beneath the lithosphere in the upper mantle. At its upper limit it contains a small proportion of molten silicates, hence its plasticity, and is largely (60 percent) formed of the mineral olivine, along with pyroxene and garnet. The temperature is around 1300–1400° C with pressures of the order of 40 kbars. These temperatures are mainly caused by the heat given off during the disintegration of the natural radioactive elements that exist in the earth, like potassium, uranium, and thorium.

Although on a short time-scale (measured in seconds) the physical properties of the mantle (seismic, for example) are those of a rigid solid; on a sufficiently long time-scale (a geological time unit: a million years) the mantle is plastic and undergoes phenomena of convection. The lithosphere takes part in these movements, it is broken up into pieces—the "plates"—that are displaced in relation to each other at speeds varying from less than 1 to more than 7 inches per year. Three relative movements are possible at plate boundaries: separation, convergence, or sideways slip. Most terrestrial volcanism is associated with the separation or convergence of plates.

An opening—created by the distension of the plates—generates a depression, which, through pseudo-adiabatic decompression, brings about the melting of a fraction of the upper mantle and the formation of a basaltic magma. This magma injects itself through vertical fissures (dikes) into the superficial 3 to 6 miles of the crust and spreads out on the surface of the active central part of the distended ridge, the rift, whose width may attain 7 miles. Submarine basaltic lava gives rise to particular volcanic forms called pillows. This formation of new lithospheric plates, or generation of new oceanic floor, occurs mostly through accretion of hot material at the plate edge, near the axis of the rift.

The ridges correspond to the uplift of two plates at the rift. In the axial part, when the plate is young or still being formed, its edges of the plates are hot, and hence lighter, compared with older zones, which are cold and heavier, and sink downward. So the region is called an oceanic spreading ridge. It is about 600 miles wide, its crest at an average depth of 8000 feet below the surface.

The ridges form a chain of more than 35,000 miles around the globe. This is the planet's most important volcanic system: In fact virtually the whole of the ocean floor (two-thirds of the earth's surface) is constituted of basaltic volcanic rocks that have been emitted during the last 200 million years from the spreading ridges. Only two spreading ridges are on land: Iceland and the Afar Depression in East Africa.

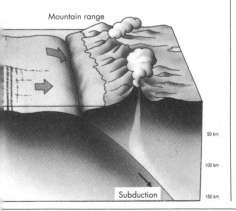

Mountain range

50 km

100 km

Subduction

150 km

Volcanism of the Subduction Zones

The convergence of two plates is the principal cause of the formation of mountain chains and of sub-aerial volcanism. There are several possible types of convergence:

Convergence of Two Oceanic Plates
In this case one plate passes under the other and plunges into the mantle. This is the phenomenon known as subduction, and brings about the formation of volcanic island arcs. Examples include the Lesser Antilles, the Marianas, the Kurils, the Aleutians, and Tonga. This is the situation under which Mount Pelée and Soufrière (Guadeloupe) were formed.

Convergence of an Oceanic Plate and a Continental Plate
In this case the oceanic plate, being denser, passes under the lithosphere supporting the continental crust and also plunges into the mantle. This results in the formation of the volcanism of cordilleras. Two examples are the Andes and Indonesia. This, too, is a phenomenon of subduction. In this way, the amount of oceanic plate consumed by subduction equals that generated at spreading ridges. The deformation and friction within the downgoing plate bring about seismicity (earthquakes) down to a depth of about 450 miles. On contact with the mantle there is reheating, and part of the subducting material melts and produces andesitic (corrosive) magma. This is the principal origin of the volcanism of the arcs and cordilleras such as the Pacific's "ring of fire." These volcanoes are characterized by their explosive eruptions, which result from the high viscosity and rich gas content of their

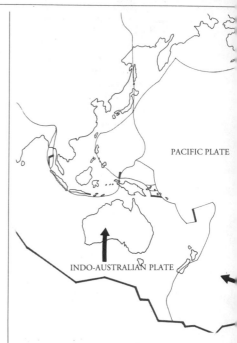

PACIFIC PLATE

INDO-AUSTRALIAN PLATE

andesitic magma. It is typical of andesitic volcanism that dormant periods may last for centuries and allow popular memory to forget. This makes these volcanoes particularly dangerous.

Finally, the confrontation of two continental plates can result in major folding that gives rise to mountain chains of the Alpine or Himalayan type. Seismicity is important here, but volcanism almost nonexistent.

Intraplate Volcanism and Hot Spots

Another cause of volcanism is linked to upwellings of hot material coming from the deep mantle, which, on reaching the base of the lithosphere, pierce it like a blowtorch. The surface expression of these columns is called a "hot spot" and

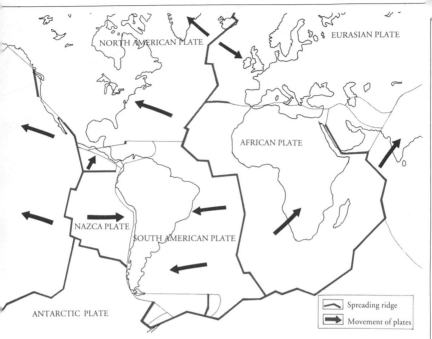

NORTH AMERICAN PLATE

EURASIAN PLATE

AFRICAN PLATE

NAZCA PLATE

SOUTH AMERICAN PLATE

ANTARCTIC PLATE

Spreading ridge

Movement of plates

The earth's tectonic plates and spreading ridges. Overleaf: The principal volcanoes.

gives rise to a volcanism whose initial magma is an alkaline, relatively fluid basalt that erupts at the earth's surface in the form of lava flows or fountains. The column is considered stationary in relation to the earth's core, and the displacement of a plate above this "blowtorch" leaves a trace on the crust in the form of strings of volcanic island chains: Hawaii and Tahiti are examples. A hundred hot spots are currently known on the surface of the globe: Hawaii, Tibesti, Tahiti, Réunion.... The active volcano of the peak of La Fournaise is also of this type. These volcanoes are of great interest to volcanologists because their frequent eruptions make them natural observatories and particularly fine sites

for perfecting surveillance methods.

Furthermore, on the ocean floor, especially that of the Pacific, there are a great number of submarine volcanic structures whose history of development is not yet well known. There are places where about a hundred—with heights exceeding 3200 feet—are found within a surface area equal to that of France.

Finally, the fissuring of some continental plates...brings about the creation of rift valleys, characterized by a special type of alkaline volcanism. These are continental rifts like the African rifts or the Rhine valley.

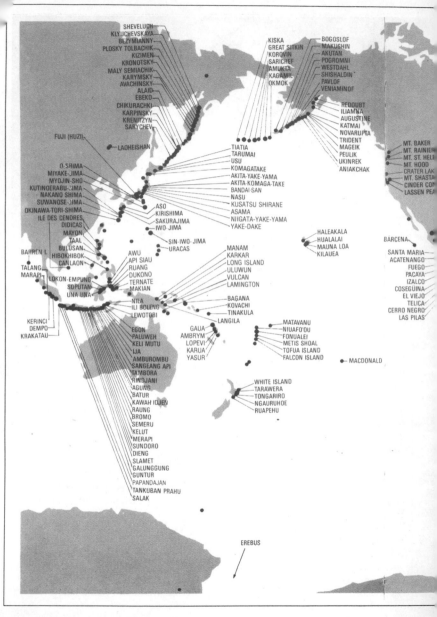

BEERENBERG

KRAFLA
SVEINAGJA
ASKJA
KVERKFJÖLL
ELDEYJAR GRIMSVÖTN
TRÖLLADYNGJA ÖRAEFAJÖKULL
HEKLA LAKI
HEIMAEY ELDGJA
SURTSEY KATLA

ISCHIA
MONTE NUOVO
VESUVIO
STROMBOLI
VULCANO
ETNA
NISYROS
GIULIA·FERDINANDEO SANTORIN

FAYAL I.
PICO I.
SÃO JORGE I.

CEBORUCO
COLIMA
PARÍCUTIN
JORULLO
POPOCATEPETL
ORIZABA
CHICHON

MOMOTOMBO
MASAYA
CONCEPCION
RINCÓN DE LA VIEJA
ARENAL
POAS
IRAZU
MT. MISERY
LA SOUFRIÈRE DE LA GUADELOUPE
MT. PELÉE
SOUFRIÈRE DE ST. VINCENT
KICK-EM-JENNY

LA PALMA I.
LANZAROTE I.
TENERIFE I.

FOGO I.

MT. CAMEROON

ERTA ALÉ
DUBBI
AFDERA ARDOUKOBA

LONGONOT
TELEKI OL DOINYO LENGAI
NYAMURAGIRA
NYIRAGONGO KILIMANJARO
MERU KARTALA

TOLIMA
PURACÉ
REVENTADOR
WOLF COTOPAXI
ALCEDO SANGAY
CERRO AZUL
FERNANDINA

EL MISTI
UBINAS
SAN PEDRO
LASCAR

SAN JOSÉ
CERRO AZUL
LLAIMA
VILLARICA
RINHUE
NILAHUE
PUYEHUE
OSORNO
CALBUCO

PITON DE
LA FOURNAISE

ST. PAUL

TRISTAN DA CUNHA

HEARD ISLAND

MT. DARNLEY

DECEPTION I.

Surveillance of Volcanic Activity and Prediction of Eruptions

The eruption of Vesuvius in AD 79 claimed about 2000 victims. If it occurred today— unpredicted and unplanned for—it would probably kill 200,000 people. The density of the populations living at the feet of active volcanoes, where soil is generally very fertile, has reached worrying proportions. It is therefore urgent that we monitor and predict the eruptions of the thousand potentially active volcanoes.

Unfortunately, there are presently only 30 or so volcanological observatories to maintain surveillance over 150 volcanoes. Fortunately, accurate predictions are becoming more numerous. Recently satellite detection has been added to the arsenal of more classical techniques.

Volcano monitoring is based on the study of the phenomena accompanying the magma's ascent. The latter produces enormous pressure that provokes fissuring (and hence seismic shocks), structural deformations (and hence measurable geometric variations), and variations in the earth's magnetic field. Moreover, gases escape from the magma and, being more mobile, they reach the surface in advance of the magma.

Understanding these parameters during the dormant period may lead to their recognition as precursors of an eruption, and thus to an accurate prediction. Furthermore, geological and volcanological study of the eruptions of volcanoes during the last few millennia allows one to reconstruct their history and to imagine various possible scenarios for future eruptions.

Seismicity and Volcanism

The boundaries between plates are the locations of intense seismicity caused by tectonic stress. Local instabilities in a volcano's magma chamber cause variations in these stresses and bring about seismic shocks within the volcano structure. The great majority of eruptions are both preceded and accompanied by seismic activity. Hence the activity of La Soufrière on Guadeloupe in 1976 was associated

Needle of Mount Pelée in 1903.

with a major seismic crisis. This type of observation enables seismology to be used as a method for predicting volcanic eruptions. It was the increase in seismicity that enabled scientists to sound the alert and then to foresee the imminence and the location of eruptions during these last few years at Piton de la Fournaise.

Each seismological station set up on the volcanoes of the Antilles and Réunion comprises a seismometer that measures the displacement of the ground caused by seismic waves. The seismometer is equipped with its own electrical power (solar panels, wind power) and a transmitter with a radio antenna that constantly transmits measurements to the observatory. In this way one can follow variation in seismic activity through time. These sensitive stations enable scientists to

detect all the little seismic shocks that precede or accompany volcanic activity, shocks too small to be felt by people.

By setting up several stations on the volcanic massif one can pinpoint the epicenters and follow the displacement of the successive seismic centers. If an earthquake, or a group of earthquakes, is recorded that is more intense than normal, the alert is sounded. If the number and extent of seismic shocks increase, a volcanic eruption may be imminent. Monitoring is then intensified throughout the network.

Deformation and Volcanism

In order to push its way through to open fissures and eject plugs of solidified lava from earlier eruptions, lava must be under great pressure. This pressure is created primarily during the injection of magma from great depths up into the magmatic chambers and

Earthquakes caused by the ascent of the magma are registered by stations surrounding Piton de la Fournaise. This allows the magmatic reservoir to be located.

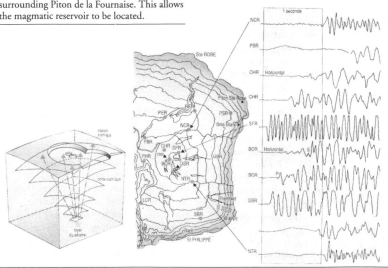

The push of magma inflates the volcano before the eruption.

reservoirs.
The pressure
deforms the structure
of the whole volcano,
"inflates" it, splits it, and modifies
its geometry before and during
the eruption. Surveillance of these
deformations therefore is the study of
variations in the volcano's geometry.
This study can be divided into two
parts: A study of the structure's overall
deformation resulting from variations
in pressure within the magma chamber
uses topographic methods and, to a
lesser extent, geophysical methods.

Monitoring of Faults
The monitoring of faults—and of the
opening of the fissures that may relate
to the region's general tectonic evolution or to the intrusion of magma—
requires local studies. This surveillance
entails methods of metrology that are
derived from those used for monitoring
of major engineering projects (dams,
tunnels, etc.), as well as geophysical
methods. The former permit
observation, to a hundredth of a
millimeter, of changes in relative

position of two points located on either
side of a fissure. The latter enable the
observer to teletransmit and record
these movements.

Both these methods are put to work
in volcanological observatories. The
peak of La Fournaise has been studied
in detail. The frequency of eruptions
there has produced an accumulation
of significant results that leads to
knowledge of the evolution of the
volcano's geometry during an eruptive
cycle. Conversely, this knowledge helps
in the prediction of eruptions.

Differential Magnetometry and Volcanism

Volcanic formations are most often
located in regions with complex
geological structures that contain faults,
aquifers, distorted zones…. These
structures considerably modify the
variations through time of the earth's
magnetic field at the surface. The
spatial distribution and extent of these

variations can be very heterogeneous. It is therefore necessary to understand in detail the magnetic signature of the volcanic massif when the volcano is inactive. To eliminate variations of the background magnetic field, scientists calculate the differences between measurements taken at the same moment at all the magnetic stations and one station chosen as the reference point. Monitoring the chronological and spatial evolution of these differences provides information about volcanic activity.

Geochemistry of Fluids and Volcanism

Magma is a bath of molten silicates that contains dissolved gases and, possibly, minerals produced by crystallization. In the magma chamber, these constituents are close to thermodynamic equilibrium at high temperature and medium pressure. The ascent of the magma and the opening of fissures produce depressurization of the upper part of the chamber. Since the solubility of the gases in the molten silicates depends directly on the pressure, this fall in pressure brings about a degassing of the magma with the creation of micro-bubbles. The formation and speed of growth of these micro-bubbles depend on numerous parameters which may include: the rate of depressurization, the speed of ascent, the viscosity of the magma, and the speed of diffusion of the constituents within the magma. The bubbles may grow to about 3 feet in size, which causes the magma to fragment.

As the solubility of the various gases is not all the same, depressurization causes a differential degassing and hence, during eruptive phases, a variation in chemical composition. The analysis of the chemical composition of volcanic gases thus provides information on the evolution of the eruptive process.

Furthermore, the topography of volcanic mountains causes heavy precipitation, especially in tropical regions. Rainfall easily infiltrates volcanic rocks, raising the water table. Underground water plays an integral role in the transfer of material resulting from volcanic activity. Hydrogeo-chemistry relies on this phenomenon for its part in volcanic surveillance.

A magmatic intrusion creates a thermal anomaly around itself. Not only does it inject heat, it also induces mobilization of chemical compounds where they are in contact with infiltrating waters. The ascent of magma is accompanied by the emission of an assemblage of volatile products (CO_2, SO_2, H_2S, alkaline halogens, etc.) which migrate along fractures. These elements meet the water table, the edifice's real lid, and partly pass into solution. The modifications in chemical composition and the temperature of springs originating below the water table are valuable indicators, the study of which enables scientists to follow the evolution of the volcano's activity. Hydrogeochemical surveillance therefore rests on measurements of physical parameters, temperature, and conductivity, as well as on chemical analyses based on regular sampling.

Geology and Volcanism

Geological research carried out within volcanological observatories is aimed at obtaining detailed knowledge of the recent eruptive history of each olcano. The past of an active volcano largely determines its future and enables the scientists to imagine possible scenarios.

There are many methods in use, including:
• collecting samples in the field; mapping the distribution of the products, eruption by eruption; compiling vertical sections of eruptive sequences;
• representative and complete sampling of the different eruptions for study in the laboratory;
• detailed petrographic study; microscopy; analyses by electron microscopy for determination of the nature of the eruptive products;
• geochemical study; chemical composition of major and trace elements; isotopic ratios, etc., giving information on the evolution of the magmas;
• dating of eruption sequences; carbon 14 dating on fossil woods; radioactive disequilibrium in minerals.

These methods also enable scientists to draw up detailed geological maps of the volcanoes in which their magmatic and eruptive history is represented.

Institute of Global Physics, Paris

The Hawaiian Volcano Observatory

The essential features of a volcano observatory are a volcano, an observer, and the record made by the observer. For success there are needed two things more—enthusiasm in the observer and publication of his record. It is an error to suppose that the purchase and maintenance of expensive buildings and instruments are among the first requirements. A physicist living continuously at Galapagos, or on Kamchatka, or in the New Hebrides, and keeping a diary, is a potential

Panorama de Saint Pierre vu du mouillage d
d'après un Document d'un Officier du Su

observatory. Students of volcanism the world over want to see that diary. Essentials of the record are exact places, maps and photographs, correct times, and descriptions and measurements of all volcanic and seismic events describable or measurable.

It is this matter of measurement that leads the observer to equip himself with instruments. But the object is not the instrument, it is the measurement. Many measurements may be made with a foot-rule, a thermometer, and a watch. The good observer uses these tools all the time. A transit or plane-table is only an extension of the foot-rule, a seismograph an extension of observation with the watch....

There are over four hundred more or less active volcanoes in the world not being continuously observed. Twenty or more of these are splendid natural laboratories. Such volcanoes are Stromboli in the Lipari Isles, Izalco in Salvador, Villarica in Chile, Tanna in the New Hebrides, Akutan in the Aleutian Islands, Waimangu in New Zealand, Bromo in Java, O-shima in Japan, Lassen in the United States, Colima in Mexico. Continuity of action, hot gases, frequency of ground movements, representative character and position—such are some of the qualities that make a given volcanic center attractive. It is not the highest or most famous volcanoes in a given belt that should be selected for steady work, but those that are practicable and reasonably free from danger....

One feature that is desirable is a settlement near at hand where reports

The bay of Saint-Pierre, Martinique, after the eruption of 1902.

net " le 10 mai, 48 heures après l'éruption
Marc Legrand, Enseigne de Vaisseau)

Activity on Kilauea, Hawaii, on the night of 29 June 1983.

may be published and mailed, where supplies may be obtained, and where headquarters may be made in case the volcano district itself is wild.

Generally exploration is necessary in addition to routine cataloguing of events. A place like Salvador, for example, has a dozen volcanic centers, some of which occasionally break into activity, although Izalco is the most faithful of the outlets. A volcano observatory is always striving to see underground. Hence the observing of slight tilts, or changes of temperature, or tremors, and the employment of volunteer observers among planters, school teachers, ministers, and government officials.

Any university or museum that can find a man willing to go to one of these countries and to live there and use his influence while there to promote volcanology and local seismology, will have taken the initial step in founding an observatory. Such a man is a missionary of science.

Thomas A. Jaggar
The Volcano Letter, no. 18
30 April 1925

The comparatively easy access at Kilauea to a variety of ongoing volcanic activities stimulated and encouraged experiments, ranging from the serious scientific to the decidedly frivolous. Visitors from America and Europe fried eggs in pans that rested on moving lava flows, learned how to thrust their cigarettes and Cuban cigars into hot cracks to light them (nonsmokers lit ends of sticks in the same cracks), embedded coins in small pieces of pasty rock, and scorched the edges of postcards on hot lava before the cards were mailed home....

Jaggar was amply aware that seismometry on an active volcano is quite different from that at a station that studies mainly distant earthquakes. Instrumentation provided a challenge from the beginning.... During their service the seismometers were modified and changed by the HVO [Hawaiian Volcano Observatory] staff to try to make them more suitable for use on the rim of Kilauea caldera—to be more responsive to local short-period earthquakes, volcanic tremor, and the extraordinary ground tiltings. These were the three distinctively Hawaiian geophysical phenomena Jaggar had identified by 1918.... Since the standard commercial seismometers had been tried and found wanting for the detection of short-period earthquakes, volcanic tremor, and ground tiltings, HVO turned its talents to designing and building special-purpose instruments. The most successful of these was the Hawaiian-type seismograph, in service worldwide by 1928.... Recognizing that seismometers took the continuing care of specialists, Jaggar searched for instruments of simple enough design to be "put into the hands of amateurs." His first "shock recorder," designed in 1928, did record separate east-west and north-south motions, but it "also recorded the motion of rats, kittens, chickens, cockroaches, and spiders...."

Seismographs are still the principal geophysical instruments at HVO. The electronic amplification and radio-telemetered signals of the current models would be startling to Jaggar's experiences, but not to his dreams....

Coastal areas in the Hawaiian Islands are vulnerable to seismic seawaves (tsunamis) generated by major earthquakes anywhere in the Pacific.... The tsunami of 1933 demonstrated that seismology could be used to predict the advent of such a wave and therefore to give warning to people in threatened areas.... Capt. Robert V. Woods...noticed his seismometer begin to record the arrival of a distant earthquake. The time between arrivals of the first and second different waves was about 10 minutes. [He] calculated the distance at about 3920 miles...and put the origin at the west edge of the Tuscarora Deep, east of Japan...[It was] agreed that such a quake could generate a tsunami in the Pacific...that would travel at about 440 miles an hour and arrive at the Island of Hawaii about 8.5 hours after the earthquake.... No lives were lost in Hawaii during the 1933 tsunami, thanks to the warnings issued by the Hawaiian Volcano Observatory. This appears to have been the first time that a tsunami was predicted through interpretation of seismograms—a forerunner by decades of the Pacific-wide tsunami-alert system now in place....

The Hawaiian Volcano Observatory has achieved much that Jaggar foretold. Fifty-one seismic stations radio information to the Observatory, where earthquake epicenters are located by computer within minutes after an event takes place. Electronic tiltmeters also telemeter data to HVO to give an instant report of the ground movement at various points on the active volcanoes. Other geophysical techniques have been added to these. The geochemical program that began with the early collections of volcanic gas at Halemaumau has gone on to calculate a total volcanic-gas budget for Kilauea. The Hawaiian Volcano Observatory and other institutions worldwide have made great strides in understanding how volcanoes work. This knowledge is being translated into forecasts of volcanic behavior that will reduce loss of life and property.

Russell A. Apple,
"Thomas A. Jaggar, Jr., and the
Hawaiian Volcano Observatory,"
in *Volcanism in Hawaii*, 1987

Mount Pinatubo

A major volcanic explosion occurred at Mount Pinatubo in the Philippines in June 1991. Rumors that the volcano was spewing out diamonds set local people frantically sifting through fallen ash, but the stones proved to be quartz crystals formed by the hardening of magma inside the volcano. The Pinatubo event, however, had much more serious effects.

Pumices from the violent 15–6 June eruptions of Mount Pinatubo bore anhydrite.... Eruption of the anhydrite-bearing Pinatubo magma injected an enormous SO_2-rich cloud into the stratosphere, which will probably lead to global-scale cooling at the earth's surface in the next few years, temporarily counteracting expected trends toward global warming.

In one of the largest explosive eruptions of the century, Mount Pinatubo (Luzon, Philippines) ejected some .7–1.2 cubic miles of dacitic magma...along with a large mass of gaseous sulfur.... The remarkably similar 1982 eruptions of anhydrite-bearing magma at El Chichón in Mexico were also accompanied by a large release of SO_2 to the stratosphere. The possibility that volcanic eruptions can modify the earth's climate has been discussed for more than two centuries, but until about twenty years ago it was erroneously believed that long-lived stratospheric clouds from volcanic eruptions consisted of fine ash or dust. In the early 1970s it was demonstrated that these stratospheric clouds actually consist of micrometer-sized droplets of H_2SO_4, pointing to the important part played by sulfur in linking volcanoes to climate change....

The sulfur gases...originally present in the magma are converted in the stratosphere to sulfuric-acid aerosols that cool the earth's surface by back-scattering and absorbing solar radiation. ... Cooling of some 0.3 degrees Celsius at the earth's surface was forecast to follow the El Chichón eruptions... several studies have suggested that the El Chichón aerosol could have either triggered or amplified the El Niño. The considerably larger stratospheric aerosol from the Mount Pinatubo eruptions, which is now producing brilliant sunsets in the northern hemisphere, has been forecast...to lead to global-scale cooling of 0.5 degrees Celsius in 1992–93. This should be sufficiently large to be distinguished from natural variations and from the surface heating associated with the moderate El Niño now underway in the Pacific Ocean. So the Pinatubo eruptions will therefore provide an important test of global climate models.

James F. Luhr
Nature, vol. 354, 14 November 1991

Ash covering a house on the flanks of Mount Pinatubo following the major eruptions of 15 June 1991.

Small explosion in the crater of Mount Pinatubo on 1 August 1991.

Chronology of Historic Eruptions

AD 79 | Vesuvius (Italy)
Ash fall, ash flows;
2000 deaths

1169 | Etna (Sicily)
Ash fall, ash flows;
15,000 deaths

1586 | Kelud (Indonesia)
Mud flows;
10,000 deaths

1631 | Vesuvius (Italy)
Ash fall, ash flows;
4000 deaths

1638 | Raung (Indonesia)
Mud flows, ash flows;
1000 deaths

1669 | Etna (Sicily)
Ash fall, ash flows;
20,000 deaths

1672 | Merapi (Indonesia)
Ash flows; 3000 deaths

1711 | Awu (Indonesia)
Mud flows; 3000 deaths

1742 | Cotopaxi (Ecuador)
Mud flows; 800 deaths

1760 | Makian (Indonesia)
Mud flows; 2000 deaths

1772 | Papandajan (Indonesia)
Avalanche; 3000 deaths

1783 | Asama (Japan)
Mud flows; 1200 deaths

1783 | Laki (Iceland)
Ash flows, gas, and
famine; 10,500 deaths

1792 | Unzen (Japan)
Avalanche, tidal wave;
10,400 deaths

1815 | Tambora (Indonesia)
Ash flows, famine;
92,000 deaths

1822 | Galunggung (Indonesia)
Ash flows; 4000 deaths

1856 | Awu (Indonesia)
Mud flows;
2800 deaths

1883 | Krakatau (Indonesia)
Tidal wave; 36,000 deaths

1888 | Bandai-san (Japan)
Avalanche; 461 deaths

1892 | Awu (Indonesia)
Mud flows; 1532 deaths

1902 | La Soufrière (Saint Vincent)
Ash flows; 1500 deaths

1902 | Mount Pelée (Martinique)
Ash flows; 28,000 deaths

1902 | Santa Maria (Guatemala)
Ash flows; 1000 deaths

1919 | Kelud (Indonesia)
Ash flows; 51,100 deaths

1931 | Merapi (Indonesia)
Ash flows; 1369 deaths

1937 | Tavurvur and Vulcan
(New Guinea)
Ash flows, base surges;
505 deaths

1951 | Lamington (New Guinea)
Ash flows; 2942 deaths

1951 | Hibok-Hibok (Philippines)
Ash flows; 500 deaths

1963 | Agung (Indonesia)
Mud flows, ash flows;
1184 deaths

1980 | Mount Saint Helens
(United States)
Ash fall, ash flows;
60 deaths

1982 | El Chichón (Mexico)
Ash fall, ash flows;
3500 deaths

1985 | Nevado del Ruiz (Colombia)
Mud flows; 22,000 deaths

1986 | Nyos (Cameroon)
Emission of
carbon dioxide gas;
1700 deaths

1991 | Pinatubo (Philippines)
Ash flows, mud flows,
and disease;
435 deaths

Further Reading

Adams, F. D., *The Birth and Development of the Geological Sciences*, Dover, New York, 1990

Alfano, G. B., and I. Friedlaender, *Die Geschichte des Vesuv*, K. Höhn, Ulm, Germany, 1929

Allen, E. T., and Arthur L. Day, *Hot Springs of the Yellowstone National Park*, Carnegie Institution, Washington, D.C., 1935

Anderson, Tempest, and John S. Flett, *Report on the Eruptions of the Soufrière, in St. Vincent, in 1902...*, Philosophical Transactions of the Royal Society, London, 1903

d'Aubuisson de Voisins, J. F., *Traité de Géognosie*, Levrault, Paris, 1828, 1834, 1835

Berthelon, Abbé, *De l'Electricité des Météores*, Bernuset, Lyon, France, 1787

Blong, R. J., *Volcanic Hazards: A Sourcebook on the Effects of Eruptions*, Academic Press, Orlando, Florida, 1984

Bory de Saint Vincent, Jean Baptiste Geneviève, *Essais sur les Isles Fortunées et l'Antique Atlantide ou Precis...Canaries*, Baudoin, Paris, 1803

————, *Voyage dans les Quatre Principales Iles des Mers d'Afrique*, Buisson, Paris, 1804

Bowen, Norman L., *The Evolution of the Igneous Rocks*, Dover, New York, 1956

Breislak, Scipio, *Voyages Physiques et Lithologiques dans la Campanie*, Dentu, Paris, 1801

Brun, Albert, *Recherches sur l'Exhalaison Volcanique*, A. Kündig, Genève et A. Hermann & Fils, Paris, 1911

Brydone, M., *Voyage en Sicile et a Malte*, Pissot Libraire, Paris, 1775

Buch, Leopold von, *Description Physique des Iles Canaries (Physical Description of the Canary Islands)*, Levrault, Paris, 1836

————, *Gesammelte Schriften*, Georg Reimer, Berlin, 1867

Buffon, Comte de, *Oeuvres Complètes*, Pillot, Paris, 1829

Bullard, Fred M., *Volcanoes of the Earth*, 2nd rev. ed., University of Texas Press, Austin, 1984

Charbonneau, Jean, *Indonésie, Montagnes de Feu*, Sudestasie, 1988

Cuvier, Georges, *Recueil des Eloges Historiques*, Firmin Didot Frères, Paris, 1861

Dana, James D., *Characteristics of Volcanoes*, repr. of 1872 ed., Reprint Services Corp., Irvine, California, 1992

Darwin, Charles, *Geological Observations on the Volcanic Islands and Parts of South America Visited During the Voyage of H.M.S. Beagle*, AMS Press, New York, 1972

Decker, Robert W. and Barbara, *Volcanoes*, W. H. Freeman and Company, New York, 1989

————, *Mountains of Fire: The Nature of Volcanoes*, Cambridge University Press, England, 1991

Decker, Robert W., Thomas L. Wright, and Peter H. Stauffer, *Volcanism in Hawaii*, U.S. Geological Survey Professional Paper 1350, Washington, D.C., 1987

Desmarest, Nicolas, *Mémoire sur l'Origine et la Nature du Basalte à Grandes Colonnes Polygones*, Mémoires de l'Académie Royale des Sciences, Paris, 1771

————, *Mémoire sur la Détermination de Trois Epoques de la Nature par les Produits des Volcans*, Mémoires de l'Académie Royale des Sciences, Paris, 1775

Dollfus, A., and E. de Mont-Serrat, *Missions Scientifiques au Mexique et dans l'Amerique Centrale, Voyage Géologique dans les Républiques de Guatemala et de Salvador*, Imprimerie Impériale, Paris, 1868

Dolomieu, Déodat de Gratet de, *Voyage aux Iles de Lipari, Fait en 1781...*, Académie Royale des Sciences, Paris, 1783

————, *Mémoire sur les Iles Ponces et Catalogue Raisonné des Produits de l'Etna*, Cuchet, Paris, 1788

Duff, J. Wight and Arnold M., *Minor Latin Poets II* (including full translation of *Aetna*), Harvard University Press, Cambridge, Massachusetts, 1935

Dufrenoy, Armand, and Elie de Beaumont, *Mémoires pour Servir à une Description Géologique de la France, Tome IV: Recherches sur les Terrains Volcaniques des Deux Siciles...*, Levrault, Paris, 1838

Ellenberger, F., *Histoire de la Géologie, des Anciens à la Première Moitié du XVIIe Siècle*, Technique et Documentation-Lavoisier, Paris, 1988

Faujas de Saint-Fond, Barthélemy, *Recherches sur les Volcans Eteints du Vivarais et du Velay (Researches into the Extinct Volcanoes of the Vivarais and the Velay)*, Nyon Aîné, Paris, 1778

————, *Minéralogie des Volcans (Mineralogy of Volcanoes)*, Cuchet, Paris, 1784

————, *Voyage en Angleterre, en Ecosse et aux Iles Hebrides (A Journey Through England and Scotland to the Hebrides)*, Jansen, Paris, 1797

Fenton, Carroll Lane and Mildred, *The Story of the Great Geologists,* Ayer Co. Pubs. Inc., Salem, New Hampshire, 1945

Ferrara, Francesco, *Descrizione dell'Etna con la Storia delle Eruzioni...,* Presso Lorenzo Dato, Palermo, Italy, 1818

Forshag, William F., and Jenaro Gonzalez, *Birth and Development of Parícutin Volcano, Mexico,* U.S. Geological Survey Bulletin 965, Washington, D.C., 1956

Fouqué, Ferdinand-André, *Santorin et Ses Eruptions,* G. Masson, Paris, 1879

Galanopoulos, George A., and Edward Bacon, *Atlantis: The Truth Behind the Legend,* Bobbs-Merrill, Indianapolis, 1969

Geikie, Sir Archibald, *The Founders of Geology,* repr. of 1897 ed., Dover, New York, 1962

Gemmellaro, Carlo, *La Vulcanologia dell'Etna, Atti dell'Accademia Gioenia di Scienze Naturali,* vol. XIV, Catania, Italy, 1858

Gesner, Konrad von, *De Rerum Fossilium, Lapidum et Gemmarum Figuris,* Zurich, 1565

Gohau, Gabriel, *A History of Geology,* Rutgers University Press, New Brunswick, New Jersey, 1990

Griggs, Robert F., *The Valley of Ten Thousand Smokes,* National Geographic Society, Washington, D.C., 1922

Guettard, Jean-Etienne, *Mémoire sur Quelques Montagnes de France Qui Ont Eté des Volcans (On Certain Mountains in France That Were Once Volcanoes),* Mémoire de l'Académie Royale des Sciences, Paris, 1752

Hamilton, William, *Campi Phlegraei (The Phlegraean Fields),* Naples, Italy, 1776

———, *Supplement to the Campi Phlegraei,* Naples, Italy, 1779

Hartung, Georg, *Die Azoren in Ihrer Ausseren Erscheinungen und nach Ihrer Geognostischen Natur,* Engelmann, Leipzig, Germany, 1860

Hochstetter, F. von, *Geologie von Neu-Seeland,* Novara Expedition Kaiserlich-Königlichen Hof-Wien, 1864

Humboldt, Alexander von, *Kosmos: Essai d'une Description Physique du Monde,* Gide, Paris, 1859

Hutton, James, *Theory of the Earth,* Messrs. Cadell Junior and Davies, London, 1795

Jaggar, Thomas A., *Volcanoes Declare War,* Paradise of the Pacific, Honolulu, 1945

———, *Origin and Development of Craters,* Geological Society of America, Memoir 21, 1947

Johnston-Lavis, Henry James, *Bibliography of the Volcanoes of Southern Italy,* University of London Press, England, 1918

Junghuhn, Franz, *Java,* Arnold, Leipzig, Germany, 1854

Kircher, Athanasius, *Mundus Subterraneus,* Janssonio Waesbergiana, Amsterdam, 1678

Koto, Bundijiro, *The Great Eruption of Sakurajima in 1914,* Journal of the College of Science, Tokyo Imperial University, vol. 38, no. 3, 1916

La Condamine, Charles-Marie de, and Pierre Bouguer, *La Figure de la Terre (The Form of the Earth),* Charles-Antoine Jombert, Paris, 1749

Lacroix, Alfred, *Figures de Savants,* Gauthier-Villars et Cie, Paris, 1932

———, *Le Volcan Actif de l'Ile de la Réunion et Ses Produits,* Gauthier-Villars, Paris, 1936

Le Hon, H., *Histoire Complète de la Grande Eruption du Vesuve de 1631,* C. Muquardt Editeur, Brussels, Belgium, 1866

Lipman, Peter W., and Donal R. Mullineaux (eds.), *The 1980 Eruptions of Mount Saint Helens, Washington,* U.S. Geological Survey Professional Paper 1250, Washington, D.C., 1981

Luce, J. V., *Lost Atlantis: New Light on an Old Legend,* McGraw-Hill, New York, 1969

Lyell, Charles, *The Principles of Geology,* Murray, London, 1830–3

MacDonald, Gordon A., *Volcanoes,* Prentice-Hall, Englewood Cliffs, New Jersey, 1972

Mecatti, Giuseppe Maria, *Raconto Storico-Filosofico del Vesuvio...,* di Simone, Naples, Italy, 1752

Mercalli, Giuseppe, *I Vulcani Attivi della Terra,* Ulrico Hoepli, Milan, Italy, 1907

Michel, Robert, *Les Premières Recherches sur les Volcans du Massif Central (XVIIIe-XIXe Siècles) et Leur Influence sur l'Essor de la Géologie,* Symposium J. Jung, "Géologie Geomorphologique et Structure Profonde du Massif Central Français," Plein Air Service, Ed. Scientifiques, Clermont-Ferrand, France, 1971

Montessus de Ballore, Comte de, *Ethnographie Sismique et Volcanique,* 1923

Montlosier, Comte de, *Essai sur la Théorie des Volcans d'Auvergne,* Landriot et Rousset, Riom et Clermont, France, 1802

Moro, Anton-Lazarro, *De Crostacei e Degli Altri Marini Corpi che si Truovano Suimonti (Crustaceans and Other Marine Bodies Found in Mountains),* 1740

Omori, Fusakichi, *The Usu-san Eruption and Earthquake and Elevation Phenomena,* Bulletin of the Imperial Earthquake Investigation Committee, vol. V, no. 1, Tokyo, 1911

———, *The Sakura-Jima Eruptions and Earth-*

quakes, Bulletin of the Imperial Earthquake Investigation Committee, vol. VIII, no. 3, Tokyo, 1916

Oviedo y Valdes, G. F. de, *Historia General y Natural de las Indias Occidentales,* repr. of 1535 ed., Madrid, 1855

Paliotti, Vittorio, *Il Vesuvio, Una Storia Scottante,* Azienda Autonoma di Soggiorno, Cura e Turismo, Naples, Italy, 1981

Palmieri, Luigi, *The Eruption of Vesuvius, in 1872...,* Asher & Co., London, 1873

Perret, Frank A., *The Vesuvius Eruption of 1906, Study of a Volcanic Cycle,* Carnegie Institution, Publication no. 339, Washington, D.C., 1924

———, *The Eruption of Mt. Pelée 1919–1932,* Carnegie Institution, Publication no. 458, Washington, D.C., 1935

———, *Volcanological Observations,* Carnegie Institution, Publication no. 549, Washington, D.C., 1950

Playfair, John, *Illustration of the Huttonian Theory of the Earth,* repr. of 1802 ed., Dover, New York, 1964

Pliny the Younger, *Letters,* translated by William Melmoth, revised by W. M. L. Hutchinson, 1927

Raffles, Thomas Stamford, *The History of Java,* John Murray, London, 1830

Raspe, Rudolph E., *An Account of Some German Volcanoes and Their Production,* Lockyer Davis, London, 1776

Recupero, Giuseppe, *Storia Naturale e Generale dell'Etna, Della Stamperia della Regla Universita degli Studi,* Catania, Sicily, 1815

Rittmann, Alfred, *Volcanoes and Their Activity,* Wiley, New York, 1962

Sainte-Claire Deville, Charles, *Voyage Géologique aux Antilles et aux Iles de Ténériffe et de Fogo,* Paris, 1848

Sarjeant, William A. S., *Geologists and the History of Geology, an International Bibliography,* Macmillan Press, London, 1980

Sartorius von Waltershausen, Wolfgang, *Uber die Vulkanischen Gesteine in Sicilien und Island,* Verlag des Dieterichschen Buchhandlung, Göttingen, Germany, 1853

———, *Der Aetna,* Wilhelm Engelmann, Leipzig, Germany, 1880

Schmidt, Julius J. F., *Vulkanstudien, Santorin 1866 bis...,* 1880

Schneer, Cecil J., *Toward a History of Geology,* M.I.T. Press, Cambridge, Massachusetts, 1967

Scrope, George Julius Poulett, *Memoir on the Geology of Central France Including the Volcanic Formations of Auvergne...,* 1827

———, *Volcanoes,* 1862

Seebach, Karl von, *Uber Vulkane Centralamerikas, Abhandlungen der Königlichen Gesellschaft der Wissenschaften zu Göttingen,* Bd 38, Göttingen, Germany, 1892

Simkin, Tom, and L. McLelland Siebert, *Volcanoes of the World,* Smithsonian Institution–Hutchinson Ross Pub. Co., Stroudsburg, Pennsylvania, 1981

Simkin, Tom, and Richard S. Fiske, *Krakatau 1883: The Volcanic Eruption and its Effects,* Smithsonian Institution, Washington, D.C., 1983

Smythe, G. W., *Views and Description of the Late Volcanic Island off the Coast of Sicily,* Joseph Booker, London, c. 1831

Soulavie, Abbé Giraud, *Histoire Naturelle de la France Méridionale,* Quillau et Merigot, Paris, 1782

Spallanzani, Abbé Lazare, *Voyages dans le Deux-Siciles...,* Emanuel Haller, Berne, Switzerland, 1795–6

Steininger, Johann, *Die Erloschenen Vulkane in der Eifel am Niederrheine,* Florian Kupgerberg, Mainz, Germany, 1820

Stommel, Henry and Elizabeth, *Volcano Weather, the Story of the Year Without a Summer, 1816,* Seven Seas Press, Newport, Rhode Island, 1983

Stubel, Alphons, *Die Vulkanberge von Ecuador,* A. Asher, Berlin, 1897

Symons, G. J., *The Eruption of Krakatoa, and Subsequent Phenomena,* Harrison & Sons, London, 1888

Thera and the Aegean World II (Proceedings of the Second Thera Congress), Thera and the Aegean World, London, 1978

Thera and the Aegean World III (Proceedings of the Third Thera Congress), The Thera Foundation, London, 1990

Thorarinsson, Sigurdur, *Hekla, A Notorious Volcano,* Almenna Bokafélagid, Reykjavík, Iceland, 1970

Thoroddsen, T., *Island, Grundriss der Geographie und Geologie,* Gotha, Justus Perthes, 1905–6

Time-Life Books Editors, *Volcano,* Time-Life, New York, 1982

Torre, Giovanni-Maria Della, *Histoire et Phénomènes du Vésuve (History and Phenomena of Vesuvius),* Jean-Thomas Hérissant, Paris, 1760

Trevelyan, Raleigh, *The Shadow of Vesuvius,* The Folio Society, London, 1976

Troil, M. de, *Lettres sur l'Islande,* de l'Imprimerie de Monsieur, Paris, 1781

van Rose, Susanna, and Ian F. Mercer, *Volcanoes,* Harvard University Press, Cambridge, Massachusetts, 1991

Velain, Charles, *Description Géologique de*

Presqu'Île d'Aden, le l'Île de la Réunion, des Îles Saint-Paul et Amsterdam, Typographie A. Hennuyer, Paris, 1878

———, *Les Volcans,* Gauthier-Villars, Paris, 1884

Verbeek, R. D. M., *Krakatau,* Imprimerie de l'Etat, Batavia, 1886

Vigée-Lebrun, Elisabeth, *Souvenirs,* 1879

Vitaliano, Dorothy B., *Legends of the Earth, Their Geologic Origins,* Indiana University Press, Bloomington, 1973

Werner, Abraham Gottlob, *Von dem Ausserlichen Kennzeichen der Fossilien (On the Exterior Characteristics of Fossils),* 1774

Westervelt, William D., *Hawaiian Legends of Volcanoes,* Charles E. Tuttle, Boston, Massachusetts, 1963

Williams, Howell, and Alexander R. McBirney, *Volcanology,* Freeman, Cooper and Co., San Francisco, 1979

Winchilsea, Earl of, *A True and Exact Relation of the Late Prodigious Earthquake and Eruption of Mount Aetna,* T. Newcomb in the Savoy, 1669

Wright, Thomas L., and Takeo J. Takahashi, *Observations and Interpretation of Hawaiian Volcanism and Seismicity 1779–1955: An Annotated Bibliography,* University of Hawaii Press, Honolulu, 1989

Zittel, Karl von, *History of Geology and Palaeontology to the End of the Nineteenth Century,* Walter Scott, London, 1901

INTERNATIONAL JOURNALS OF VOLCANOLOGY

Bulletin of Volcanology, IAVCEI, Rome, 1874–97, 1924–31, 1937–40, 1949–84

Bulletin of Volcanology, Springer, Berlin, 1986–

Journal of Volcanology, Berlin, 1914–38

Journal of Volcanology and Geothermal Research, Elsevier, Amsterdam, 1976–

Volcano Letter, Hawaiian Volcano Observatory, 1925–55

BOOKS BY KATIA AND MAURICE KRAFFT

A l'Assaut des Volcans, Islande-Indonesie, Presses de la Cité, Paris, 1975

Au Coeur de la Fournaise, Editions Roland Bernard, Saint-Denis, La Réunion, 1986

Dans l'Antre du Diable, Volcans d'Afrique, Canaries et Réunion, Presses de la Cité, Paris, 1981

La Fournaise, Editions Roland Bernard, Saint-Denis, La Réunion, 1977

Guide des Volcans d'Europe, Delachaux et Niestlé, Neuchâtel, Switzerland, 1974, 1991

Les Plus Beaux Volcans d'Alaska, en Antarctique et Hawaii, Solar, Paris, 1985

Questions à un Volcanologue: Maurice Krafft Répond, Hachette, Paris, 1981

Volcano, Abrams, New York, 1975

Volcano!, Young Discovery Library, Ossining, New York, 1992

Volcanoes: Earth's Awakening, Hammond, Inc., Maplewood, New Jersey

Volcans du Monde, Flammarion-Odyssée, Paris, 1987

Volcans et Dérive des Continents (new edition of *Notre Terre, une Planète Vivante,* published in 1978), Hachette, Paris, 1984

List of Illustrations

Index

Photograph Credits

Text Credits

B Maurice Krafft was born on 25 March 1946.
A volcanologist and geologist by training,
.68 he and his geochemist wife, Katia, founded the
..ch Centre de Volcanologie Vulcain, which specialized
in the phenomenology of volcanic eruptions. Over
nearly a quarter of a century they visited hundreds of
volcanoes and observed almost 150 eruptions around
the world. They were the authors of a score of books and
five films on volcanism and also assembled the largest
volcanological library in the world and an important
collection of volcanic pictorial material. Both Maurice
and Katia Krafft died while photographing the
eruption of Unzen in Japan on 3 June 1991.

Translated from the French by Paul G. Bahn

Project Manager: Sharon AvRutick
Typographic Designer: Elissa Ichiyasu
Cover Designer: Robert McKee
Editorial Assistant: Jennifer Stockman
Design Assistant: Penelope Hardy

Library of Congress Catalog Card Number: 92–82807

ISBN 0–8109–2844–2

Copyright © 1991 Gallimard

English translation copyright © 1993 Harry N. Abrams, Inc., New York,
and Thames and Hudson Ltd., London

Published in 1993 by Harry N. Abrams, Incorporated, New York
A Times Mirror Company

Printed and bound in Italy by Editoriale Libraria, Trieste